Finding Global Balance

Common Ground between the Worlds of Development and Faith

Finding Global Balance

Common Ground between the Worlds of Development and Faith

Katherine Marshall
Lucy Keough

THE WORLD BANK
Washington, D.C.

Contents

BOXES

TABLES

Saint Patrick's Hall, Dublin Castle

James D. Wolfensohn
President
The World Bank, 1995–2005

Foreword

James D. Wolfensohn
President, World Bank

For the past seven years, together with former Archbishop of Canterbury, now Lord George Carey, I have been privileged to travel a fascinating path aimed at building and strengthening dialogue between the worlds of faith and development. We have explored a wide array of issues related to poverty alleviation, social services and social justice, global security, and other facets of the global changes that affect us all today. Beginning in Lambeth Palace in 1998, with the first meeting of world faith and development leaders convened by George Carey and me, a meeting which had the notable support of His Highness the Aga Khan, and continuing to the present, when Archbishop Diarmuid Martin helped bring together these leaders, it has been a remarkable journey. This work has attracted a growing number of patrons, participants, and advocates, and has evolved into a worldwide network—unlike any other—of leaders from major world faith traditions and major financial and development organizations. Since the Lambeth meeting, this group has gathered three times: in Washington, D.C., in 1999; in Canterbury, England, in 2002; and, most recently, in Dublin, Ireland, early in 2005.

Between these historic meetings, the work of the partnership has been pursued by a modest organization, the World Faiths Development Dialogue (WFDD). Together with efforts from the World Bank, we have worked to foster engagement between development institutions and faith leaders and communities. The WFDD engaged, for instance, with the Bank during the preparation of the *World Development Report 2000/2001: Attacking Poverty*, gathering inputs from more than 200 people around the

world, and bringing important faith perspectives to the WDR. Within the
World Bank, we have worked to forge strategic partnerships with key interfaith and faith organizations. Among those, two have been especially
prominent. First is a dialogue, now some two years old, among the World
Bank, the International Monetary Fund, and the World Council of
Churches aimed at airing differences and finding common ground in
approaches to fighting poverty. Second is a growing partnership with the
Community of Sant'Egidio, an impressive Catholic lay organization that
works in a variety of countries in a host of development areas, including
an HIV/AIDS treatment program in Mozambique.

I feel deeply the importance of the partnership between faith and development for many reasons. It has helped me—and, I believe, the World
Bank—to view many of the critical development issues that we confront
on a daily basis from a different and enriched perspective. The world of
faith leaders and communities brings keen insight into the daily lives of
poor people: faith leaders are often the most trusted people in their communities, in many cases providing social services, not only to the people
who espouse their same beliefs but also to the community as a whole.
Faith leaders have longstanding and consistent on-the-ground experience,
often working steadfastly despite extreme conditions. They thus have a
deep and complex perspective to offer. In many cases, they can help bring
the voices of the poor to the table in powerful ways. Listening and learning from faith communities throughout the world has helped me—and
has great potential to help the World Bank as a whole—appreciate that
material development must be complemented by other less-tangible
aspects of development: community cohesion, choice and opportunity to
reach one's potential, and core values that define the moral and spiritual
underpinnings of individual and community welfare. Truly translating the
mission of the World Bank—to help bring about a world free of poverty—
into successful and sustainable improvements in people's lives requires
taking these aspects into account.

During the past few years, the world has been rocked by a series of
tumultuous events. We continue to see and feel the repercussions of the
tragedy of September 11, 2001. Since that time, many other countries have
suffered other attacks of terrorism that were designed to divide and de-
stabilize our world. Natural disasters—from floods in Central America, to

earthquakes in Iran, to the recent dreadful tsunami in Asia—have caused havoc, destruction, and death in affected communities. The combination of these events underscores the challenge to all of us to confront global poverty, inequity, and mounting social tensions as primordial threats to global security.

It is my strong conviction that the partnership among faith leaders and organizations, governments, and development organizations is vital to the efforts to address the challenges confronting today's world. Quite simply, we share similar missions and motivations, and our work will be much more effective if we collaborate. We know that, in many countries throughout Africa, faith-based organizations represent perhaps half of the health and education services; in the more remote areas that may have been isolated by civil conflict, faith-based organizations are often the *only* source of health and education. The faith contribution across a wide span of HIV/AIDS interventions in Africa is undeniable. Whereas the efforts of faith communities have long been acknowledged in Latin America, other parts of the world also have dynamic and evolving relationships with faith communities that provide social services. There is much to explore in these areas. There is, I believe, room for partnership on the ground and certainly much to learn from each other. Faith communities are critical partners if we, in the international community and the development community in particular, are to succeed in reaching the Millennium Development Goals.

Like many international financial institutions, the World Bank has been rather slow to recognize and pay tribute to religious and faith leaders and communities who work on development. This approach has begun to change, although it has proved challenging to develop appropriate and durable institutional approaches within the World Bank itself. Moreover, some faith leaders have been slow to recognize the commitment and contributions made by the World Bank and other international development institutions. However, countries have now begun to reach out to faith communities as part of their outreach within the Poverty Reduction Strategy process, recognizing that theirs is a trusted voice for local communities to channel their hopes and priorities to government decision makers. Professionals across many disciplines within the World Bank are recognizing more and more that faith leaders and communities are important partners. It has been, admittedly, quite difficult to translate these insights and experiences into action, primarily because the World Bank's mission requires us to work, first and foremost, through country governments. There is thus a continued challenge in deciding how to negotiate relationships with civil society organizations in general and with faith communities in particular. But we must explore creative ways to engage in these partnerships, balancing the operational mandate of the World Bank with the need to reach more widely and inclusively into communities to understand their development needs.

We gathered in Dublin as my tenure as president of the World Bank was drawing to a close. As I look back at my years at the Bank, I fervently hope the work of these years will translate into a better, brighter future for the World Bank's clients, the countries themselves, and most particularly the poorest of the poor. In looking back on how I have invested my energies over the years, I am pleased that we have come so far together (though still with so far to go) in building this partnership between the Bank and faith leaders and communities to strengthen and reinforce mutual trust and to bring about more effective results for our clients. It is an area, I believe, that holds tremendous potential for our work of creating a world free of poverty. We have myriad challenges ahead, and we will be better prepared to address them if we work together. For myself, I am fully committed to continuing this essential collaboration.

Greetings
Bono

Where you live should not decide, whether you live or whether you die.
—"Crumbs From Your Table"

Bishop Gunnar Staalsen
 I write this note on my back
with a prolapsed disc. when I should
be greeting you to my home town in
person ... I hope everybody at this
Faith and Development conference knows
just how important a role the
churches have to play .... I have been
amazed at what has happened in the
United States with the most conservative
denominations .... they listened, they learned
and when the sleeping giant woke up
they really went to work ... on HIV AIDS
on inequality etc... The church has a a
chance to redescribe itself for a new
generation of skeptics by placing
'extreme poverty' as the greatest moral
challenge of the age your fan Bono

god to see you at DAVOS

Archbishop Diarmuid Martin

Lord George Carey

Preface

Development and Human Dignity

Lord George Carey and
Archbishop Diarmuid Martin

Development is about people. It is about people with fundamental needs but also with fundamental rights; with unalienable dignity; and with remarkable imagination, creativity, potential, and capacity. Development is about real people in concrete situations. It is about people in the poorest regions of the world. It is about the survivors of natural disasters, such as the recent devastating Asian tsunami. It is about people in war zones. It is about people with HIV/AIDS. It is about people who hunger daily, who have no access to clean water. It is about children who work when they would love to go to school and parents who cannot give them minimum health care. It is about all the other reasons that people throughout the world are poor and marginalized and yet still manage to hold out hope for a better future for themselves and their children. Development is about human potential—the extraordinary potential that is in each person, a potential that is so compromised by poverty.

We—religious leaders and leaders of international development and financial organizations, businesses, and civil society—came together in Dublin, inspired by our commitment to strengthen and scale up the global fight against poverty and social injustice. We are joined by a common desire to reinforce our bonds with poor people, who may lack political voice but who possess one great towering asset: their human dignity. We have both traveled the globe and witnessed people, young and old, who are sometimes in conditions of tremendous distress and deprivation but who, nevertheless, cherish hopes and dreams, for themselves, for their children, for their loved ones. We have seen women and men, who may lack economic and food security, but who day by day show remarkable initiative and resourcefulness in going beyond hope to ensure that their children are healthy and happy, go to school, and enjoy a better life. In the Christian tradition, we say that they dream of being able to realize the image of God that is in them, a God who loves and wants each person to realize the potential within. Other faith traditions espouse similar sentiments. Most fundamentally, we share a common dream to eliminate poverty, to allow people to determine their own futures, and to realize a world marked by equity and security.

The remarkable partnership between the worlds of faith and development on which this volume is based has a fascinating history. Shortly after Jim Wolfensohn became president of the World Bank, he contacted a number of religious leaders with the objective of launching a dialogue between the World Bank and other development organizations and the world's faiths. Recognizing that the arenas of faith and development shared a wealth of experience and a passionate commitment to eradicating poverty but had very limited experience in collaborating, Jim Wolfensohn invested considerable energy in bringing these two worlds together.

The result was a historic gathering of faith and development leaders at Lambeth Palace in 1998. The meeting provided an extraordinary vehicle for each "side" to share, with remarkable candor, its concerns about the mission and motivation of the other. Not surprisingly, because faith communities had traditionally been among the most vocal opponents of the World Bank, they leveled much of their criticism at the Bank. Faith and development communities spoke different languages and had many misgivings and many misunderstandings about each other. This rocky start could easily have caused us all to turn back, to revert to our respective "corners." And yet it did not. What drew us together was more resilient than what had kept us apart. The strong consensus that emerged from the meeting was to continue to build bridges and to search for common ground for future cooperation.

Since Lambeth, we have seen this partnership grow in numbers and in strength, and the dialogue branch out into new areas. We are deeply convinced of the value of this work: faith and development constituencies can learn much from each other, and we must do so if the battle against poverty and social injustice is to be won. On the one hand, we believe that there is a deeper appreciation within the corridors of the World Bank and other international financial institutions of the need for a more holistic, values-based approach to development that takes greater account of the social and spiritual underpinnings of poor communities. On the other hand, there is also greater recognition within many faith organizations of the economic parameters of growth and development. With humility, we suggest that our work over the past seven years has contributed to this greater understanding.

But the challenges that lie ahead—of eliminating poverty, expanding access to health care, ensuring universal primary education, combating the dreadful scourge of HIV/AIDS, and forging a more peaceful and secure world—are daunting and remind us daily of the need to recommit ourselves to this partnership. We have long seen that religious traditions of all kinds work directly with poor people throughout the developing world. As significant providers of social services—health, education, and HIV/AIDS—faith-based groups have developed an intimate sense of how poor people live; of their needs, hopes, and aspirations; and of how economic development could best serve those needs. We must constantly challenge ourselves—as a group and as individuals: how can we tap into and marry the extraordinary energies and networks of both the faith communities and the traditional development agencies to better respond to the needs of the world's poor?

As a group, we have committed ourselves to fulfilling the Millennium Development Goals—targets for eradicating extreme poverty and hunger; achieving universal primary education; promoting gender equality and empowering women; reducing child mortality; improving maternal health; combating HIV/AIDS, malaria, and other diseases; ensuring environmental sustainability; and developing a global partnership for development. At this writing, the realization of many of these goals for the world's poorest countries remains doubtful. Reaching them will hinge on making significant investments in creative partnerships and finding new ways to tackle poverty. Collaboration across the worlds of faith and development stands as a prime example of such fresh approaches.

As we look toward the future, there is much to do. Plans are afoot to relocate and restructure the World Faiths Development Dialogue, the small agency that has been the institutional mechanism for many faith and interfaith groups to structure their dialogue with the World Bank. Our aim is to sharpen the focus of what we can realistically do together and to serve as a focal point and place of connection for development and faith leaders around our common concerns.

Our objective is to work together to eliminate basic economic poverty and the worst forms of social injustice within our lifetimes—to create the environment whereby every woman, man, and child can realize their full human potential, taking full advantage of their talents and gifts as active protagonists within the human family and the global community. To do this, we must be humble enough to know we cannot do it alone. We must stay focused on partnership, on striving to understand the lives of the poor and how they can improve, and on how we can bring the resources of our institutions to bear on this, the greatest challenge facing the world today.

Participants assembled in St. Patrick's Hall, Dublin Castle

(l to r) Lord George Carey, James D. Wolfensohn, His All Holiness Ecumenical Patriarch Bartholomew, Archbishop Diarmuid Martin

From Lambeth to Dublin—Seeking Global Balance

With a central mission to address global poverty and inequity, a group of world leaders from faith communities and key development organizations met in Dublin in late January 2005. This was the fourth meeting since the first such group, convened by Jim Wolfensohn and then-Archbishop of Canterbury George Carey, met at Lambeth Palace early in 1998. Over this period, the world saw momentous changes. The global landscape withstood a series of tumultuous events that have shaken human consciousness and renewed the urgent desire among many people to confront mounting social tensions and widespread poverty as fundamental threats to world security.

Relentless images of the December 2004 tsunami gave new meaning to catastrophe and suffering. They came on top of stories of misery throughout the world, equally great though less concentrated and less visible: the simmering tragedies of conflict in Iraq, Darfur, and elsewhere; widespread disease (including, but far from limited to, the HIV/AIDS pandemic); natural disasters—floods, mudslides, and hurricanes—that left a trail of devastation and posed a daunting challenge for rebuilding and restoration; and inadequate water, widespread hunger, and failing schools. Poverty and security seemed more tightly linked than ever before, posing dual threats to economic and social welfare and reviving muted debates about the need for social justice and equity. The annual World Economic Forum

at Davos, Switzerland, in late January 2005 surprised many as it cata-
pulted poverty to the top of its agenda, while the World Social Forum in
Porto Alegre, Brazil, the same month, echoed urgent calls to "make poverty history" as the centerpiece of global priorities.

The combined repercussion of these phenomena lends urgency to
long-planned initiatives to revitalize the global commitment to fighting
poverty set out in the 2000 Millennium Declaration and the Millennium
Development Goals (MDGs; see p. xxvi). At a profound level, the conflu-
ence of events showed a world that is marked by myriad complexities and
deep inequities—a world far out of balance. The global community has
accepted the MDGs as a shared responsibility and has designated 2005 as
the "year of development." A UN Summit in September 2005 will take
stock of progress on those goals. Yet, several far-ranging assessments
already suggest that the MDGs are not on track,[a] indicating the need for
more focused attention on what needs to change, as well as what more
needs to be done, to progress more rapidly. Realization of the original
goal motivating this partnership of faith and development leaders—to
combat global poverty—thus remains illusive.

The first meeting of faith and development leaders, at Lambeth Palace in
February 1998, established shared concern about the challenge of poverty
but highlighted many gaps in understanding. A second meeting, in Washington, D.C., in November 1999, moved toward establishing working partnerships. The third meeting, at Canterbury in October 2002, bound the
effort more tightly to the global agendas reflected in the Millennium Development Goals and set five priorities for action: HIV/AIDS, gender, education, health, and conflict. The fourth meeting, in Dublin in early 2005,
took stock and reset the course. This meeting, where Archbishop Diarmuid
Martin joined Jim Wolfensohn and Lord Carey as cohosts, had special
meaning, coming near the conclusion of Jim Wolfensohn's tenure as president of the World Bank and thus focusing on the future direction of the
partnership.

---

a. Two of these are "Investing in Development: A Practical Plan to Achieve the
Millennium Development Goals," the report from the UN Millennium Project led
by Professor Jeffrey Sachs (New York: Earthscan, 2005 [http://www.unmillennium
project.org/reports/index.htm]), and *Global Monitoring Report 2005* (Washington,
D.C.: World Bank, April 2005).

Held in historic St. Patrick's Hall of Dublin Castle (see box), the gathering of some 60 participants included former Irish President Mary Robinson; Prince Turki Al-Faisal Al-Saud of Saudi Arabia; Indian Sikhs; senior clerics of the Jewish, Catholic, Anglican, and Christian Orthodox religions; Buddhist monks and a Shinto priest; Islamic scholars; Irish NGOs; philanthropists; private businesspeople and academics; and leaders from a number of development organizations. Noteworthy was the participation of His All Holiness Ecumenical Patriarch Bartholomew, whose visit to Ireland was the first in history for an ecumenical patriarch.

HISTORIC DUBLIN CASTLE

The Dublin meeting of world faith and development leaders took place in St. Patrick's Hall of Dublin Castle, a site with special significance in Irish history. King John of England ordered Dublin Castle built in 1204 "for the administration of Justice and the custody of treasure" of his Norman colony. The city of Dublin takes its name from Dubh Linn or Black Pool, on the grounds of the present Castle Gardens.

The castle served as the center of British rule until 1684, when it burned completely in a fierce fire fueled by an enormous tower filled with gunpowder. When the castle was rebuilt in 1750 as a Georgian palace, it once again became the headquarters of British rule in Ireland. The Easter Rebellion of 1916 marked the beginning of the end of British rule, while the signing of the Anglo-Irish Treaty in December 1921 ended seven and a half centuries of colonial rule. In 1922, with the creation of the Republic of Ireland, Dublin Castle became the heart of government of an independent nation, surviving the subsequent civil war and the transition to Irish nationhood. A restored castle stands today as one of the preeminent examples of Georgian architecture in Ireland, with St. Patrick's Hall used for numerous government functions, including the inauguration of Irish presidents.

The haunting strains of an Irish low whistle called each session to order with elegance and poignancy. Aptly launched, the Dublin group addressed a wide gamut of issues over two days, all with global import and impact. Prominent among them were responses to and lessons from the recent Asian tsunami, where faith organizations have played a vital role in relief efforts; moral and ethical issues around HIV/AIDS; gender and youth; and the roots of conflict—all viewed through the lens of equity. The central imperative of putting a dignified human face on all approaches to development was a recurring theme. In the words of Archbishop Diarmuid Martin, "Development is about real people, people in concrete situations. . . . They possess one great asset, their dignity." People also live their lives in the context of the natural environment and spiritual values.

The meeting stressed the vital need for greater harmony and balance in today's world. Coming soon after the December 2004 tsunami, the world's generous outpouring of support for the tsunami victims contrasted with daily indifference to still larger tragedies of hunger, HIV/AIDS, and widespread unemployment and exclusion from opportunity. For many, this contrast harkened to what Jim Wolfensohn has termed a *world out of balance*, where millions lack access to safe water, where children die from entirely preventable diseases, where child labor is endemic at the sacrifice of childhood and basic education, and where access to drug therapy to treat HIV/AIDS is highly inequitable. Allusions to the ethical dimensions of fighting poverty were peppered throughout almost every debate, with many speaking to the need for moral foundations for equitable and sustainable development.

The impending close of Jim Wolfensohn's term as president of the World Bank put the discussion of this faith/development partnership at a crossroads, and a key aspect of the agenda was the future path for this group of faith and development leaders. Over this seven-year period, this fledgling partnership has evolved and matured. The scope of dialogue about how to fight poverty together and more effectively has deepened, in line with a commitment to break down the walls that have separated these two worlds that care so deeply about eradicating poverty and enhancing social justice. The network of leaders composing this group has grown, and friendships within the group have strengthened. The meetings, in turn, have explored critical global policy issues and practical efforts to address them. This process has enhanced understanding, trust, and empathy among important institutions and people, and has helped pave the road toward stronger collaboration across these two constituencies.

Efforts to exchange views and to work together have encompassed a kaleidoscope of activities. Among the more prominent has been establishing and nurturing the World Faiths Development Dialogue (WFDD), which supports the effort to translate the insights, sense of common purpose, and practical ideas of this group of leaders into action on the ground.

This book tells the story of this partnership within the context of the Dublin meeting. It draws primarily on background materials prepared for the meeting and on discussions during the meeting itself. The participants share an obvious bond in their desire to address global poverty and inequity, and they are eager to set benchmarks for collaboration. We hope this book does justice to their rich, candid, and provocative deliberations.

Millennium Development Goals

In September 2000, the largest gathering of world leaders in history came together at the United Nations Millennium Summit. The Summit's final declaration, signed by 189 countries, committed the international community to an agenda of poverty reduction, consisting of eight Millennium Development Goals (MDGs).[a] The following MDGs are widely recognized as benchmarks for improving international development.

Goal 1. Eradicate extreme poverty and hunger.
- ∾ Halve, between 1990 and 2015, the proportion of people whose income is less than one dollar a day.
- ∾ Halve, between 1990 and 2015, the proportion of people who suffer from hunger.

Goal 2. Achieve universal primary education.
- ∾ Ensure that, by 2015, children everywhere—boys and girls alike—will be able to complete a full course of primary schooling.

Goal 3. Promote gender equality and empower women.
- ∾ Eliminate gender disparity in primary and secondary education, preferably by 2005, and in all levels of education no later than 2015.

Goal 4. Reduce child mortality.
- ∾ Reduce by two-thirds, between 1990 and 2015, the under-five mortality rate.

Goal 5. Improve maternal health.
- ∾ Reduce by three-quarters, between 1990 and 2015, the maternal mortality ratio.

Goal 6. Combat HIV/AIDS, malaria and other diseases.
- ∾ Have halted by 2015 and have begun to reverse the spread of HIV/AIDS.
- ∾ Have halted by 2015 and have begun to reverse the incidence of malaria and other major diseases.

Goal 7. Ensure environmental sustainability.
- ∾ Integrate the principles of sustainable development into country policies and programs, and reverse the losses of environmental resources.
- ∾ Halve by 2015 the proportion of people without sustainable access to safe drinking water.

---

a. World Bank website on the Millennium Development Goals: http://ddp-ext.worldbank.org/ext/MDG/home.do.

∽ By 2020, achieve a significant improvement in the lives of at least 100 million slum dwellers.

Goal 8. Develop a Global Partnership for Development.

∽ Develop further an open, rule-based, predictable, nondiscriminatory trading and financial system.

∽ Address the special needs of the least-developed countries.

∽ Address the special needs of landlocked countries and of small island developing states.

∽ Deal comprehensively with the debt problems of developing countries through national and international measures in order to make debt sustainable in the long term.

∽ In cooperation with developing countries, develop and implement strategies for decent and productive work for youth.

∽ In cooperation with pharmaceutical companies, provide access to affordable essential drugs in developing countries.

∽ In cooperation with the private sector, make available the benefits of new technologies, especially information and communications.

What of the Progress on the Millennium Development Goals?

In September 2005, world leaders will gather to assess the progress and to recommit themselves to achieving the MDGs by 2015.

Much work is needed. *Partnerships in Development, Progress in the Fight Against Poverty*[b] found that uneven progress was being made in terms of meeting the Millennium Development Goals. The report notes that if current trends in growth and poverty reduction continue, the goal for eradicating extreme income poverty on a global level is within reach. But additional resources and progress, at the level of specific countries, will be needed if this goal is to be met for all countries. Moreover, this goal may well be the only one to be fully realized, because for many of the other goals—such as achieving universal primary education, promoting gender equality, and reducing child mortality—current rates of progress are too slow.[c]

---

b. Washington, DC: World Bank, 2004.

c. See also World Bank, *Global Monitoring Report 2005, Millennium Development Goals: From Consensus to Momentum* (http://siteresources.worldbank.org/GLOBALMONITORING EXT/Resources/complete.pdf), and "In Larger Freedom: Towards Development, Security, and Human Rights for All," Report of the Secretary General, 21 March 2005 (http://www.un. org/largerfreedom/report-largerfreedom.pdf).

ॐ

His All Holiness Ecumenical Patriarch Bartholomew
and Archbishop Diarmuid Martin

Diversity, Compassion, and Social Harmony

His All Holiness
Ecumenical Patriarch Bartholomew

D ifferences between natural beings are essential to life and are what create harmony of the world, just as differences in musical pitch create harmony in a musical composition. All relationships—between young and old, between men and women, between coreligionists and believers in another faith, between indigenous and alien, between rich and poor—should be founded on such mutual harmony and complementarity.

Any organism is composed of various elements, each one performing a different function, so that their totality keeps the entire organism alive. In human society, vanity and egotism can upset this harmony of vital functions. When individual cells in a body—or when members of a society—are led astray by selfish concerns that work against the common welfare and that seek to expand to the detriment of the rest, a cancerous growth is formed that leads to the demise of the organism.

Evil is raucous and seeks to impress and to lead astray by a pretense of force. By contrast, people of God and spirituality can be mild, gentle, and effective in doing good. This goodness is reflected in the many elements of benevolent forces evident within the body of society. A prime example can be found in the experience of a survivor from the horrors of the concentration camps of Nazi Germany, where brutality and death reigned supreme. This man confirmed his fundamental optimism in the goodness of mankind when he wrote that, in spite of all the horror he had experienced, he still felt that humanity is not a black sheet with occasional white blots of goodness but, on the contrary, a white sheet of goodness with occasional black blots of evil. Truly, our societies hide vast reserves of love and decency, most recently demonstrated by the many large and small contributions to alleviate the sufferings of the victims of the recent earthquake and tsunami in Southeast Asia. This generosity is, indeed, hopeful and gives us assurance that our own efforts will not be rendered ineffective.

Still, we cannot remain complacent. The entire tenor of our society remains too much influenced by self-centeredness and its triptych of branches: personal ambition, avarice, and lust. We see, on a daily basis and extolled in the mass media, too many examples of unbridled competition, vainglory, and the pursuit of celebrity. This situation should not fill our hearts with disappointment but rather with the urge to act; to act in common; and to reject these standards of self-love in favor of the adoption of godly love, charity, and contribution—in other words, those objectives that underlie this meeting in Dublin.

We should recognize how these selfish standards contribute to the rise of conflict. Conflict is deleterious. It absorbs energy and hampers productivity. It destroys progress, often wrought with much effort. It causes poverty rather than wealth. Even when there is unequal distribution of wealth founded on injustice, conflict is not the path to social harmony, but to still more social upheaval.

It is equally erroneous to think it is possible for social peace to prevail when there is a deficit of social justice. When social wealth is justly allocated, progress is achieved in tandem with peace and prosperity for the masses.

The most extreme example of social desperation in today's world is terrorism. By generating hope and by satisfying reasonable demands, we can disperse desperation. For the struggle against terrorism to have any hope of success, its weapons must be, not firearms, but love, compassion, and the elimination of poverty and of social injustice.

Let us hope, brothers and sisters, that our societies will succeed in eliminating poverty and conflict so all the world can live a happier life. May it be so.

Participants arrive at Dublin Castle; in the foreground His All Holiness Ecumenical Patriarch Bartholomew and Gregorios Yohanna Ibrahim, Archbishop of Aleppo

Cardinal Theodore McCarrick and Rabbi David Rosen

CHAPTER 1

The Many Dimensions of Equity

In a world of shared information, with the poorest of the poor in many countries recognizing Bollywood or Hollywood stars, people today, more than ever before, have a vivid view of the vastly unequal ways in which the people of the world live. The lives of the rich and the poor are documented, and each can see how the other group lives. Everything is well known and well seen. Everybody knows or can know everything. The rich part of the world knows what is happening in the poor part of the world, and they know what is happening in our part of the world. That means that the poor, the unfortunate, and the poor nations know very well what we are doing or not doing. Inequity is visible and its reality can never be avoided.

—Mario Giro

The central premise and core challenge of the Dublin meeting was a keen awareness that the world is dangerously out of balance. Amid great plenty for many, some 1.2 billion people live on less than $1 a day, and close to 3 billion live on less than $2 a day. In an era of spectacular health advances, more than 40 million people are HIV positive, yet less than a fraction have access to life-saving drugs, so that more than 3 million people died of AIDS in 2004. With outstanding education the norm in many parts of the world, still more than 115 million children are not even in school—two-thirds of them girls and one-third with disabilities. These brutal and frightening numbers paint a picture of great misery and premature death, and they vividly portray the inequity and missed opportunities that poverty entails.

All who met at Dublin Castle shared a common commitment to confronting this harsh reality: that billions of people live in poverty and thus have little opportunity to develop their potential or even lead a decent life. All, with one voice, described fighting poverty as the greatest challenge facing humanity. The Dublin meeting followed close on the heels of two global meetings that same month: the World Social Forum in Porto Alegre, Brazil, and the World Economic Forum in Davos, Switzerland. Poverty rose to the top of the agenda in all three settings, as many individuals and groups, from very different parts of the world and different sectors of activity, affirmed both the imperative and their determination to work together to find new ways of confronting poverty. Lagging progress on many of the Millennium Development Goals (MDGs)—reflected in a series of recent global reports—spurred this focus. Bishop Gunnar Staalsett highlighted the common challenge to confront the situation and to build on today's remarkable potential for global consensus and global action. As a first step, he said, we need to probe deeper into the challenges of poverty. He asked, "What can we learn if we listen to the differing perspectives symbolized by Davos, Porto Alegre, and Dublin?"

Father Dominic Peccoud posed an alternative question, "What is different at this meeting, which involves people from faith communities?" His answer, echoed in many forms, is that faith communities regard the dignity of each individual as a lodestar: "We need to consider how the poorest people can be at the center of their own development. The heart of development is not leaders meeting to discuss opportunities, but people taking action to change their lives." Hearing "the voices of the poor"—to ensure fulfilling the MDGs and to ensure equity—was, therefore, both a starting point and an end point for the Dublin group.[1] That philosophy echoes the emphasis on empowerment and community-driven approaches that are common among development institutions today.

The challenge before the Dublin group was not only to address the wretched living conditions of fellow human beings who lack the most basic necessities of life, but also to address tensions between equity and diversity, continuity and change, and opportunity and fairness, as well as links between inequality and instability.[2] Participants explored the implications of imbalances among societies and nations, as well as within them. They noted that citizens around the world experience profound differences, not only in living standards, but also in influence, in access to legal systems, and in power and social status. In Prince Turki Al-Faisal Al-Saud's words, "It is contrary to all the faiths that we live in such an inequitable world. Let us get it back into balance."

THE MEANING OF EQUITY

In 1946–47, during consultations on the Universal Declaration of Human Rights, a small group of philosophers and religious leaders provided substantive inputs on basic issues of human dignity and equity. Their inputs helped to highlight the common core of shared values and concerns that cross many cultural boundaries; they also acknowledged important lingering challenges and far-ranging differences. In the decades since then, major global events and vast social and economic change have challenged, elaborated, enriched, and refined these concepts. The ideas of rights and equity are closely linked, and the challenge of translating them into understandable terms and above all into action remains a leading challenge for the global community today.

More recently within development debates, links between equity, economic development, and social justice are increasingly coming under scrutiny in the search for deep and sustainable poverty alleviation. Disparities in income, abilities to meet basic needs, and access to health care and education have long been hallmarks of life for the poor and dispossessed in many developing countries, but the situation is much more starkly visible today. The effects of such disparities go far beyond physical deprivation. They are accompanied by vast differences in political influence and social status for individuals, as well as for communities. Apart from the profound ethical issues, the presence of such inequalities has many other implications and manifestations. Poverty alleviation becomes much more intractable. Crime and violence will often escalate. The ultimate consequence is that institutions (both public and private) are undermined, the climate for public investment is poisoned, and the potential for social unrest increases. In other words, the fabric of society unravels.

These are extremely arduous challenges and require dialogue, partnerships, analysis, and action.

The hope for the Dublin meeting was not that the group would reflect a common view of equity or would espouse any formal position. Rather, the aim was to build an agenda on common ground, such as that presented by Hans Kung in his work toward a global ethic, and by Amartya Sen in his concept of capabilities. Hans Küng has drawn from the major world faith traditions and philosophies a common set of basic values and principles that he terms a *global ethic* and that can be viewed as a foundation for both interfaith and intersectoral dialogue. Amartya Sen, who has brought concepts of freedom and opportunity squarely to the fore in economic theory and practice, has focused global antipoverty action on the development of human capabilities and the expansion of choices. Questions before the Dublin group thus included: How strong is the common ground? Where are the areas of tension and difference? And, above all, how do reflections on equity enrich our understanding of the effort needed to attain a world free of poverty?

Different cultures, traditions, and disciplines understand equity differently. Dublin participants, therefore, concurred that they should approach the concept with caution and humility. The English word *equity* traces its roots to the Latin term *aequs,* meaning justice and fairness, and definitions commonly give *fairness* as a synonym. The term has links to systems of justice, finance, economics, and philosophy, yet it is also basic to each individual and family that grapples constantly with issues of fairness and balance among individuals and communities.

Dublin participants drew distinctions between equality and equity. Whereas individuals have different and unequal needs, preferences, abilities, and efforts, equity implies some measure of social justice and respect for personal freedom for all.

While Dublin participants easily distinguished between equity and equality, they found it more difficult to agree on a definition of equity. The metaphor of a "level playing field" proved useful but left lingering questions: What opportunities does each person need to have an equitable chance at life? Do common definitions of equity suggest certain types of policy prescriptions? What role do safety nets play in ensuring equity?

Evolving concepts of equity have paralleled the evolution of legal, judi-cial, moral, and theological thinking and systems. Moreover, this concept is increasingly spotlighted in development policies and practices as having an important bearing on sustainable and just economic progress. (Box 1.1 below suggests some perspectives from the experience of Ire-land.) Equity in some definitions is tied to rights to property; in eco-nomics the notion has helped move dialogue and analysis beyond distributing benefits toward broader ideals of a just society. Above all, equity speaks to the need for social justice and the idea of a "social contract" and social rights.

BOX 1.1. IRISH HISTORY AS A METAPHOR

Ireland offered a suitable backdrop for a meeting on fostering equity and eradicating poverty. Ireland's rapid transformation from a lower- to a higher-income country provides inspiration and hope for what development can achieve. Ireland's example shows that countries can drastically shift positions in the global community, and that prosperity can be redistributed among countries, as well as within a single country.

Irish history serves as a metaphor for what we are doing here today. A hundred years ago, the notion of a senior Irish Catholic prelate and a senior Church of England prelate jointly hosting a gath-ering at Dublin Castle—the epicenter of British rule—would have been derisibly absurd. Irish history helps us understand faith as an inspiration for development and humanitarian work. Throughout the twentieth century and even earlier, Ireland was the center of a sig-nificant missionary movement that left its mark not only on religious life but also on educational traditions. Today, nongovernmental Christian organizations like Trócaire and Christian Aid have earned a reputation for both their dedication and their professionalism.

Ireland's official Development Cooperation Program has drawn on Catholic and Protestant sources as a wellspring of inspiration,

(Continued)

BOX 1.1. (Continued)

thus promoting education, equality, and human rights, as well as combating poverty, exclusion, and disease. People with religious views must take a position on the world's lasting problems, particularly those related to development, thus ascribing to religious leaders, like political leaders, a huge moral imperative. The Millennium Development Goals are not just a sound, worthy, noble idea but a time frame—an action plan—within which we are all expected to actually achieve results.

We in political leadership in Ireland and elsewhere in the world expect and hope that religious leaders will keep us under pressure with regard to achieving the MDGs. We expect you to be vocal. We expect you to be extremely critical if we fail to achieve those goals in both a domestic and an international context.

In his report titled "Investing in Development,"[3] Professor Jeffrey Sachs concludes that national strategies for achieving the MDGs require the involvement of civil society—including, I would add, faith-based organizations. Civil society organizations can help reduce poverty by focusing attention on the goals and the actions required to achieve them.

When one looks at the MDGs, one could be forgiven for saying that they appear daunting. However, again, I reaffirm that we have a clear target. Let us keep everybody under pressure to achieve the intentions laid out in front of the world. It would be catastrophic if we were to arrive at the year 2015 without achieving these goals. The effect on the United Nations and the UN-based system—which we in Ireland cherish—would be much worse than the divisions opened by the Iraq war. If these brave targets are not achieved, the public will be much more cynical about the United Nations than perhaps ever before in its history. It should be a shared goal for us all in the realms of both politics and faiths.

—Conor Lenihan

EQUITY AND FAITH TRADITIONS

Every faith tradition has grappled with equity. It is a core principle of Jewish law, a backbone principle of Islam, and a central element of the foundations of Christianity. The Baha'i tradition focuses on equity in many of its teachings, as does Buddhism, both emphasizing the mutual responsibilities of both rich and poor in societies where outcomes vary so widely. Charity, in its many forms, has also been central to faith traditions and has been associated closely with equity. Yet some faiths have accepted the notion—historically reasonable—that poverty is inevitable. For these traditions, the contemporary goal of a world without poverty and with far more egalitarian societies requires an evolution in thinking.[4]

Rabbi David Rosen recounted a discussion in the Midrash (the two-millenia-old homilectical exposition of the Bible) by two great Jewish sages of the time, Rabbi Akiva ben Yosef and Rabbi Ben Azai, on the most important part of the Bible. Rabbi Akiva held that most important principle is "and you shall love your neighbor as yourself" (Leviticus 19:18). Rabbi Ben Azai argued for the notion of the human individual as created in the divine image (Genesis 5:1). According to Rosen, "Akiva was saying that you can love your neighbor only if you can appreciate the divine image within yourself, as well as within your fellow human being. Enhancing awareness of the dignity and divinity within every person is at the heart of realizing human potential. It is, therefore, essential in overcoming the travesties of inequity."

Rabbi Rosen also cited the biblical concept of the sabbatical year as an important aspect of equity. Such a year—which occurs every seven years—includes three important elements: debt relief, release from bondage of anyone who is completely controlled by others, and sustainable development through conservation of arable resources. Rabbi Rosen noted, "This wisdom—the ancient wisdom of the sabbatical year—is perhaps more crucial for our well-being today than ever before."

The biblical concept of a covenant, Rosen held, is also fundamental to equity. "The sanctity of the individual is always in creative tension with the value of community and collective responsibility. Today, when the blessing of individualism is often transmuted into greed, avarice, and egomania, ideas about a covenant—which different religious traditions frame in different ways—have much to teach modern society about living in harmony with the earth and its natural resources, and about ensuring social justice."

Bishop Gunnar Staalsett contended that the Commandments—the greatest laws in the Judeo-Christian tradition—are similarly relevant to global justice. The Commandments address a world in which the rich steal from the poor by overexploiting resources that are rightfully theirs, where millions die of hunger not because the world lacks food but because it is unfairly distributed, and where rampant corruption in government and business puts what should rightfully go to the poor in the hands of the rich. "These traditions," said Bishop Staalsett, "which people often interpreted as applying only to individuals, are also corporate and political, in that politics is the instrument by which we order a just world."

Prince Turki Al-Faisal Al-Saud noted that he wished that friends who speak about Judeo-Christian traditions would add "Islamic" to the mix, because Islam has much to say about equity and about keeping everything in balance. Prince Turki noted that the great Christian and Jewish thinkers Thomas Aquinas and Maimonides based some traditions on what they learned from Muslim scholars.

Much of philanthropy stems from these traditions, since all religions speak to the responsibility of the rich toward the poor and to the concept of sharing. For example, when Muslims fast during the month of Ramadan, they are expected to show special generosity to the poor. A Jewish tradition calls for reserving a share of crop land to feed the poor—the idea being that God is the real owner of the land and reserves part of it for the poor. In Sikhism, the tradition of *langar* is central: after services, rich and poor gather to share a free vegetarian meal. In Hinduism, feeding the poor is a core virtue: the poor are to be fed during any special ceremony or occasion. Different faiths have various methods of sharing; some of those include an economic system based on reciprocal giving, as in some indigenous traditions; rules for obligatory giving, as in the Muslim *zakat*; and voluntary giving, as in many Christian traditions and in *Dana*, a pillar of Buddhist practice.[5] (See boxes 1.2, 1.3, 1.4, and 1.5 for some reflections on equity from different faith perspectives.)

INEQUITY IN AN AGE OF GLOBALIZATION

Like their colleagues in development institutions, many faith leaders and institutions are reflecting on the equity challenges presented by the global

BOX 1.2. REFLECTION ON EQUITY IN JEWISH LAW

Jewish Law defines equity as *lifnim mishurat hadin*—literally "on the inside of where the legal line is drawn." This definition implies careful compliance with the spirit as well as the letter of the law, or *din,* in contrast to the English phrase "within the law," which implies a minimum standard of compliance. "Within" implies behavior that is closer to some sacred absolute—action that tempers flaws in this less-than-perfect world and ensures justice and mercy, freedom and equality.

Examples of such behavior include observing the laws of tort with punctiliousness, and remaining silent even when hearing oneself reviled. Examples also include protecting others while forgoing protection for oneself; restoring lost property even when the owner despairs of its retrieval; and paying compensation to workers who cause damage, even if they cannot prove the absence of negligence. It is *lifnim mishurat hadin* to recognize that another person needs a contested amount more than one's own self.

—Rabbi Hillel Levine[6]

economy and the social change those challenges entail. In today's globalized world, notions of equity and justice become complex and must take into account a multiplicity of market structures and organizations and their different and sometimes contradictory impact on individuals and communities. Markets themselves must function in a world of many institutions, which are keenly affected by the presence or absence of democratic processes in a country; human and civic rights; free and open media; and access for all social and income strata to basic education, health care, and economic safety nets. We see around the world today a host of organizations that influence global actions and have global repercussions and implications. Some are clearly national in scope—largely tied to individual governments. Many others, falling into the public, pri-

BOX 1.3. "THE PEOPLE OF THE MIDDLE": THOUGHTS ON EQUITY IN ISLAMIC TRADITION

We are enjoined by God to treat each other equitably, and those are words from the Koran. Even when we are dealing with natural resources and animal life and wildlife, the injunction upon us is to be sensible and reasonable so an imbalance will not occur in the presence of those lives, including plant life.

And when the Prophet Muhammad, peace be upon him, was asked, "Who are you, Muslims?" he said, "We are a people of the middle." Of course, this means on the one hand that there is no zealotry, and on the other hand that there is no laxity.

Another verse from the Koran says that we have created everything in balance, and that this is true in everything a Muslim does and thinks, except in one thing: when we commit a sin, it is counted only once. But when we do good, it is counted in our favor ten times. And that is an expression of God's generosity to humankind.

—Prince Turki Al-Faisal Al-Saud

vate for profit, private not for profit, and "nondenominational" spheres, are international, with reach and influence that are often hard to judge, but that have widely differential effects in different parts of the world.

Within countries, people's participation in markets and economic processes—both in degree and substance—is shaped by myriad social arrangements and public policies. The sharing among different groups in the benefits of economic growth (i.e., poverty reduction or entrenchment) also depends on social institutions and on the degree to which they promote or frustrate equity.

Rabbi David Rosen took a broad approach to the moral challenges linked to globalization and the capitalist economy. He argued that capitalism has an interest in reducing global inequity, but that capitalists usually want someone else to pay for that outcome. He said that the same is true for environmental protection: "The free rider, while rational in a narrow sense, is profoundly selfish and in the end self-destructive. We need to ensure that people and states understand the shortsightedness of this position—that they see selfishness as destructive. The crucial need to develop an ethic of responsibility and thus to address the challenge of inequity cannot be left to market forces alone. This is above all an educational challenge, and one where the wisdom of faith traditions can and must play a crucial role."

In a world of shared information—where the poorest of the poor often recognize people from other corners of the earth—everyone has a first-hand view of the vastly unequal circumstances in which people live. According to Mario Giro, "The poor, the unfortunate, and poor nations know very well what the rich in rich nations are doing or not doing; this visibility and inequity can provoke violent reactions."

He recounted his encounter with a former child soldier in Uganda. "Why did you take up weapons when you were 10 years old?" he asked the youth. "I wanted what I watched on television," the youth replied. The world is becoming smaller as people everywhere have access to the same images, hear the same songs, and drink the same beverages, yet people continue to live worlds apart.

The recent tsunami brought these inequalities to the fore, with people worldwide glued to their screens and combing their newspapers for images of the devastation. The tsunami, noted Mario Giro, showed that rich and poor were dying together, but, nevertheless, underlined the deep divisions between them. Western governments focused on recovering the bodies of Westerners and preventing them from being thrown into mass graves. "Such an approach means we put a high value on each individual, but the rich also want to stress that difference," Mario Giro noted. Only a week after the tsunami, people again began returning to affected areas as tourists, claiming that they were helping local economies. "When a region reaches the point where it does not even merit a period of mourning but is instead compelled to reopen go-go bars to continue to compete in tourism, something is wrong. That says a lot about inequity."

Lord Brian Griffiths highlighted the potential of capitalism to promote growth and thus to fight poverty, noting, however, that other considerations aimed more directly at equity are also important: "Although capitalism will never produce equity, capitalism is the only way we can eradicate poverty on a global basis," he maintained. The market economy dates from the political economy of Israel in the Old Testament, where property rights rest on justice. Lord Griffiths continued, "We should be fighting for that kind of market rather than fighting against the market, because arguing against the market is just not viable." The push for corporate social responsibility has paralleled capitalist expansion, with outside and internal pressure spurring corporations to adopt codes of ethical conduct.

Meanwhile, philanthropists have moved away from charitable giving toward giving that fosters social justice and systemic change. Lord Griffiths described young colleagues who are very successful at age 40 but who are searching for significance in their lives: "They want to invest in Third World countries. They want some return, but they recognize that it does not have to be risk-adjusted return on capital, which a private market would want. I believe we must draw on those resources and put them to good use."

INTERNATIONAL CONSENSUS

For perhaps the first time in human history, a powerful consensus has developed that the global community must ensure that all people, everywhere, have a minimally decent standard of living. Every head of state at the Millennium Summit of the United Nations in September 2000 affirmed the MDGs. Again at the Monterrey conference on Financing for Development in March 2002, voice after voice professed determination to fulfill these goals by 2015. In a UN summit planned for September 2005, the global community will take stock this year—at the first five-year mark—of how it is faring in this effort.

In parallel with this consensus, there is within development circles a renewed emphasis on equity considerations as central elements in the success of poverty reduction efforts. First, unequal opportunity, as well as inferior access to schools, health facilities, roads, and markets, are themselves a source of poverty and are indications of inadequate voice, representation, and political participation. Second, the success or failure of poverty reduction efforts reflects both aggregate growth and its distribution. An important underpinning is institutions and policies that pro-

BOX 1.4. BAHA'I TRADITION: FAIRNESS AND EQUITY

Equity is fairness—the standard by which each person and group is able to maximize the development of their latent capacities. Equity differs from absolute equality in that it does not dictate that all be treated in exactly the same way. While everyone is endowed with talents and abilities, the full development of those capacities may require different approaches. Equity ensures that access and opportunity are fairly distributed so this development can take place.

Equity and justice are the twin guardians of society. Equity is the standard by which policies regarding the use of resource decisions should be made. Justice is the vehicle through which equity is applied—its practical expression in the life of an individual and a society. Only through the exercise of true justice will trust be established among diverse peoples, cultures, and institutions.

—Matthew Weinberg

mote equity across a range of sectors. The effect of growth on poverty depends on a host of additional interrelated factors across economic, environmental, financial, and social strata. Sustainable change requires more than increases in household incomes. It requires a foundation of positive social change that understands power dynamics and culture and value systems. The shape and direction of public policies and institutions has a profound impact on development.

Mary Robinson observed that the Global Governance Initiative at Davos had given all four actors on the MDGs—international institutions, governments, the private sector, and civil society—poor marks. The Initiative's 2005 report focused specifically on the private sector, giving it an average score of 3 out of 10. She saw the Dublin group as well equipped to advocate that the private sector improve its record on the MDGs and, thus, on equity. The Global Governance Initiative pointed out several areas in

BOX 1.5. SOME REFLECTIONS ON CHRISTIAN PERSPECTIVES OF EQUITY

Christianity takes a prophetic stance against systemic injustice. In addition, it has drawn on the twin fundamental doctrinal planks of incarnation (God becoming human in the person of Jesus, thus affirming the ultimate goodness of the created order) and Trinity (the idea of God conceived as three interdependent persons, reflecting community in its very nature). The coming of Jesus brings God's judgment on the world and its iniquities. While Christians are called to live under that judgment, they are also called to live according to the generous example of God shown in the living example of Jesus. "For you know the generous act of our Lord Jesus Christ, that though he was rich, yet for your sakes he became poor so that by his poverty you might become rich" (2 Corinthians 8:9).[7] Christians believe that God's Kingdom of justice and equity will ultimately prevail over any injustice in the human world. In reflecting the generosity of God's gift of himself in Christ and the community of love of the Holy Trinity in their lives, they believe that they are engaging with God to realize these two principles.

—The Reverend Canon Richard Marsh

which corporations can contribute. These areas include core business practices, new products and markets that tackle environmental challenges and deliver affordable goods and services to the poor, hybrid business and philanthropic activities such as in the context of HIV/AIDS, and strategic corporate philanthropy. The report specifically suggested actions that pharmaceutical and information technology companies could take, and it recommended transparent and responsible engagement in public policy.

Discussions at Davos linked the Global Governance Initiative report to the "quick wins"—or practical steps—suggested by the Sachs report.[8] These steps include providing free school meals for all children using locally produced foods with take-home rations; distributing free, long-lasting, insecticide-treated bed nets to all children in malaria-endemic zones; eliminating school uniform fees, which would especially enable girls to attend classes; and helping communities plant trees to provide nutrients, shade, fodder, watershed protection, windbreaks, and timber.

Mario Giro spoke for all his colleagues in calling for a culture of compassion and for overcoming the resignation that is the "social sin of the rich world. . . . Having the information, having the means, having the know-how—all of that is a gift. We will be judged on how we spend that gift, because unlike our predecessors, this generation has the opportunity to address poverty."

He pointed out the inequity often exemplified by world leaders gathering to speak about poor people and poor nations: "Remember, we are talking about real people. We have to approach our task with enormous caution, respect, and a little fear and shame."

According to Bishop Gunnar Staalsett, "After dialogue comes right action, as awareness of others compels us to live differently. . . . From encounters with people who are suffering, we need to see not only facts and figures but also faces. Our task is to translate morality, motivation, and memory into a machinery that changes the world."

NOTES

1. The *Voices of the Poor* publications by the World Bank—which include complex portraits of poverty, focus on dignity, and reveal the commonality of issues across communities and region—provided inspiration for the meeting.

2. See *World Development Report 2006: Equity and Development* (Washington, DC: World Bank, forthcoming, September 2005).

3. "Investing in Development: A Practical Plan to Achieve the Millennium Development Goals," UN Millennium Project (directed by Jeffrey Sachs), 2005.

4. The winter 2005 issue of the *Journal of Interdisciplinary History* explores historical approaches to poverty, wealth, and equity among monotheistic faiths.

5. "Poverty and Development: An Inter-Faith Perspective" (Oxford: World Faiths Development Dialogue, November 1999).

6. Professor of Religion, Boston University.

7. New Revised Standard Version.

8. See note 3.

(l to r) Douglas Balfour, Brizio Biondi-Morra, Chanel Boucher, Monsignor Frank Dewane, Hany El Banna, Ekaterina Genieva, Mario Giro

2

Tsunami Realities, Aftermath, and Lessons

When we feel another's pain and respond with intuitive wisdom and compassionate action, we catch a glimpse of the natural state of the human mind and heart.

—Sulak Sivaraksa

As the Dublin meeting opened, the tragedy of the Asian tsunami was at the forefront of global attention and was felt with particular keenness by those across the world whose primary concern is international poverty and development. Striking 11 countries just a month earlier, on December 26, 2004, the massive waves left a path of death and devastation; Indonesia, Sri Lanka, India, and the Maldives were most severely affected. Despite intense media coverage—story after story and terrifying images of destruction and suffering—the scope of the tragedy seemed beyond comprehension, a shocking reminder of the fragility of life and power of nature. This awe at the magnitude of disaster and of the poignant suffering it caused was echoed by all who met at Dublin, especially the several leaders who had just visited the hardest-hit areas.

The tsunami gripped the global community in ways that had virtually no precedent. Its severity and vast geographic reach challenged disparate groups to work together in quite new ways. The extraordinary outpouring of support and generosity of spirit across the world stood in hopeful contrast to the shattering images of devastation. In introducing the topic, Jim Wolfensohn exhorted the community "to address not only the facts of the tsunami but its significance and lasting impact. What does the political, human, ethical, moral—and faith-based—response to this terrible tragedy mean?" Why did the disaster inspire such a remarkable public and private response and extraordinary solidarity?

While the tsunami touched a wellspring of empathy and support in people around the world, it left behind large and nagging questions, comparisons, and challenges. How can we, as a global community, evoke the comparable response that is needed in light of the plight of the 700 million people who go to bed hungry every night, the millions who suffer from diseases such as HIV/AIDS and malaria, and the millions of children who are not in school? The leaders at Dublin searched for common threads that might see a replica in these "other tsunamis"— the less visible but equally devastating challenges posed by the world's poor, especially in Africa. There was hope that the event might reshape the global agenda in 2005—commonly seen as a global "year of development"—with the United Nations stock-taking summit on the Millennium Development Goals (MDGs) in September 2005, a major upcoming event, which could amplify global concerns about the challenge of poverty and shine a light on the real needs and prospects for mobilizing resources.

The Dublin group focused also on the immediate challenges ahead in the tsunami-struck areas, above all on the complex continuum of assistance needed to convert immediate relief into longer-term rebuilding. At all costs, the hidden trap of rebuilding poverty was to be avoided. It was quite clear to all that the significance of the tsunami was still unfolding, and that it would test the sustained will and commitment of all faith and development leaders assembled in Dublin.

THE SCOPE OF THE TRAGEDY

The tsunami showed little discrimination and played no favorites, washing away both poor villages and luxury resorts, both people eking out a simple living and wealthy vacationing Europeans. No faith was spared— Hindus, Buddhists, Muslims, and Christians alike suffered. Those who had visited the affected areas related their personal stories of the devastation. Towns were not destroyed; they vanished. The death toll quickly surpassed that in Hiroshima following the atomic bomb; at the time of the Dublin meeting, it stood at some 220,000. Cardinal Theodore McCarrick, recently returned from Sri Lanka, likened the force of the water to a powerful vacuum cleaner, sucking out everything in its wake. "The waves came in with such power," he said, "that the light-fitting clothes that so many people were wearing were ripped right off them. Their bodies were found nude because of the strength of the waves."

In the Indonesian province of Aceh alone, more than 150,000 died. Jim Wolfensohn related his experience visiting Indonesia, the Maldives, and Sri Lanka. He found the devastation beyond anything he had ever seen, even in post-conflict countries—"just a void, as though nothing had ever existed there before." Some anthropologists fear that some 72 indigenous tribes populating the remote Andoman and Nicobar island chains may never recover. In Chennai, India, where fishing is the basis of livelihood, boats vanished along with homes. All along the coast from India to Sumatra, the sea that had given and sustained so many, swept away lives and livelihoods, becoming a fearful threat. Even the fish disappeared for a time. The images were apocalyptic.

The impact on children—who accounted for about half the victims—was especially cruel. Because of their smaller size and lesser strength, children were unable to resist the force of the water and to cling to buildings, trees, and other structures while waiting for it to recede. Some relief groups found whole towns and villages in areas of Aceh province with virtually no children left. The trauma suffered by the surviving children can scarcely be imagined. Cardinal McCarrick related the experience of Catholic Relief Services, which had brought a child psychiatrist to Sri Lanka. The psychiatrist asked a group of children to do four drawings: how their houses had looked before the tsunami, how their houses had looked as the tsunami struck, how their houses looked after the tsunami, and how they wanted their houses to look "tomorrow." Though the purpose of the exercise was healing through constructive work with memory and hope, it was also revealing of the lodestars of the children's worlds and of how they had shifted with the tragedy. Jim Wolfensohn suggested that the children's analysis was a good metaphor for the financial, economic, and human reconstruction that is the task of development organizations such as the World Bank.

Master Sheng Yen pointed to the need for relief efforts to help the young people who have lost parents and family to find a place to live and finish their education. The task of searching for missing family members presents a Herculean challenge. Thoraya Obaid reminded the group, "We should not assume that all these children are orphans." Even where parents have been killed, an extended family structure may protect a child against, for example, the evils of child trafficking. Hany El Banna also highlighted the real dangers of child trafficking, when so many children and families are so vulnerable.

Lorna Gold pointed to the transformative impact on children in countries not directly affected: "There is a sense of urgency and a desire to seize a historical moment. Children, in particular, have begun to understand the difference between what I want, and what I need, and what other people need."

The needs of women should never be ignored—as they have been too often in disaster situations—cautioned Thoraya Obaid. "One particular always falls between the cracks, and that is the essential needs and dignity of women in times of war or natural disaster. Birth is forgotten, but birth happens, whether during war or peace. Too often humanitarian assistance fails to recognize the specific biological needs of women—their monthly cycle, miscarriages—and that decreases their dignity. Each stage of assistance should consider these needs."

Events that seemed like miracles occurred alongside the devastation. A baby was found after several days floating on a mattress off the coast of Thailand. In India, people reported that an eight-year-old boy sat up in the midst of a mass burial. A three-year-old fisherman's son from northeast Thailand, torn from his mother's grasp when the waves struck, was found in a treetop in a mangrove forest after three days. But these isolated examples of hope could not mask the scenes of death and destruction.

Equally miraculous, perhaps, has been the dignity and resilience of tsunami victims. Cardinal McCarrick told of encountering these qualities among young and old alike in Sri Lanka. In one village, fishermen told government and aid workers, "Don't give us food. Don't give us money. Just fix our boats, and we'll go out and start working again. We will be able to feed our families, and we will have jobs. Please just fix the boats."

Thoraya Obaid described this response as "more than resilience. It is the desire to regain dignity."

THE GLOBAL RESPONSE

The outpouring of money, goods, prayers, and compassion from around the world has no parallel in recent history. Sulak Sivaraksa observed, "The greatest act of generosity in the history of the world has followed the most massive natural catastrophe in recent memory. This outpouring of human compassion has rippled across this fragile planet, opening the hearts of people from every nation, every spiritual tradition, and every race."

Cardinal McCarrick agreed: "The generosity that the tsunami has evoked in the civilized world has been remarkable." Billions of dollars have been pledged in official government aid. Military support was made widely available to distribute relief supplies. Teams of military doctors patrolled some of the most affected areas, dispensing care and medicines and also monitoring outbreaks of communicable diseases. Multilateral aid agencies cut through red tape, making funding readily available for both emergency relief and reconstruction. UN agencies quickly established an on-the-ground presence. The World Food Programme has plans to feed some 2 million people per month for at least six months. Non-governmental organizations (NGOs) came to the forefront of relief efforts almost instantly after the last wave receded. The World Bank has engaged from the first day in mobilizing its resources and, above all, its networks.

Perhaps most remarkable is the extraordinary response of individuals to the tsunami, and underneath that response is a new sense that millions of people have shouldered this challenge as their own responsibility. World Vision reported record levels of fundraising, much of it unsolicited. Many people not affiliated with any group simply wanted to help neighbors and strangers in need. More than 6 million people made direct contributions to UNICEF, reported Phillip O'Brien. Churches, temples, and mosques around the world all reported record fundraising campaigns within their congregations. Hany El Banna marveled that Islamic Relief had received "incredible levels of contributions"—then totaling some $20 million—"from Mormon churches, Christian organizations, Ameri-

can organizations, Sikh temples, Hindu temples, and Buddhist groups."
He suggested that the most exciting repercussion was the degree to which
the tragedy revealed massive individual willingness to assume responsibility for global challenges that could ultimately translate into a deeper
sense of collective social responsibility.

Religious organizations and leaders of all faiths—Muslim, Catholic,
Jewish, Quaker, Anglican, and Buddhist, to name a few—have joined
forces in the relief effort. Special food packages are being sent to widows
in Sri Lanka who are observing the Iddah period of mourning. Catholic,
Anglican, Jewish, and Hindu organizations have been unfailingly ready
with both material and spiritual support, thereby feeding and sheltering
the homeless, providing health services, helping bury the dead in keeping
with local traditions, and offering prayer and counseling services. Sulak
Sivaraksa's story was representative:

> Innumerable acts of courageous compassion immediately followed the dis-
> astrous events that took place on Koh Phra Thong, the Golden Buddha
> Island, in the southern part of Thailand. Siamese and foreign women risked
> their lives to carry dozens of children to higher ground as monstrous moun-
> tains of water smashed onto the shore. This instinctual response to protect
> the children shows that the heart often does respond selflessly and coura-
> geously in the face of harm. Nearly every Buddhist temple in southern Siam
> was transformed into a relief center to take care of the living and the dead
> from all faiths and nationalities. As many who suffered through this
> tsunami now recognize, fearlessness in the face of danger and suffering is
> the source of liberation of the soul.

Many people stressed that spiritual and psychological rebuilding is at
least as important as physical reconstruction. Jim Wolfensohn observed
that "in many ways human reconstruction will be the most difficult," and
that faith communities will have a special role to play.

Thoraya Obaid suggested that the psychological toll on women who
have lost children will be especially heart-wrenching. "We have already
seen from Aceh, some women—mothers who have lost one or two or three
children—who are tying to commit suicide." Compounding this pain will
be the "guilt that she let go of the child. That kind of trauma will stay with
women for a very long time and require special psychological treatment."

Philip O'Brien noted, "However difficult it will be to rebuild the thousand or more schools in Aceh, making sure that no woman wakes up screaming because she remembers she has lost a child—and that no child wakes up screaming because the waters are coming again"—will be even more difficult.

Dr. Patricia Nickson noted that "counseling is very important initially, but it will be much more important when people regain their normal— or relatively normal—lives. From my own experience of observing genocide and massacres in Africa, the real trauma hits maybe three months later, sometimes longer."

SEARCHING FOR EXPLANATIONS

A tragedy on the scale of the Asian tsunami inevitably drives people to search for explanations. Many at Dublin were posing difficult questions: Why did it happen? Why has the global community responded with such extraordinary solidarity and support? What can we learn from this experience that can mobilize people to respond to other global crises? Participants offered clues, some rooted in spiritual traditions. Many spoke of compassion as a bedrock of many religious traditions. Sulak Sivaraksa pointed to the Buddhist philosophy that "beneath our habits and belief systems, beneath our attachments and opinions, beneath our fear of other people, beneath different credos and opposing political philosophies, we are basically good, with compassion our core nature."

Rajwant Singh cited the belief of Guru Nakak, the founder of the Sikh faith, that one of the most basic elements of Sikhism was compassion, noting Sikhs felt this to be a prerequisite to a connection to God. Many would ask, in the days ahead, whether the challenges humankind poses to environmental sustainability contributed in any fashion to the catastrophe.

There were references to the state of moral decline in the world, not in any causal sense but, nonetheless, highlighting that many saw the disaster as a wakeup call, a warning against excessive concentration on materialism and self-interest. Swami Agnivesh pointed to what he saw as a "spiritual deafness and blindness that has overtaken" the world. "Gone are the days when God-awareness was natural and intimate to human consciousness, when God could speak in the still small voice of love and communion. . . . Indulgence dulls our sensitivities, especially our spiritual sensitivity. When hearts of flesh turn into hearts of stone, it takes a hammer blow to make any kind of impact." (See box 2.1.)

Sulak Sivaraksa brought into the discussion the Buddhist philosophical view of humankind's innate goodness and intuitive wisdom and compassion:

> Deep within our souls, we can feel our connection to the world around us, but we have lost touch with both our myths and our spiritual call. We so frequently abuse those around us and misappropriate nature's resources for our own advantage in the name of self-gain and profit. . . . But the heart of compassion remains a single moment away from our present self-gratifying habits. As we have witnessed in the past few weeks, our pure heart will not lie dormant in the face of human tragedy. . . . This tragedy has reawakened the passion and joy of life within many.

Others concurred with the proposition that, however catastrophic, the tsunami has reshaped the psychological landscape of the West.

While no one pretended to offer any firm answers to the "why" questions, all the faith leaders rejected the notion of the tragedy as divine punishment for worldly transgressions. Faouzi Skali noted that religious leaders have a responsibility to help their congregations understand that "if you say it is a punishment, it means that people deserved the punishment. They did not. They did nothing, especially the children. Religious leaders have to explain and show solidarity."

Cardinal McCarrick proffered the idea of "the mystery of God's providence" in the world. "When I was little we learned that you do a tapestry from the back; you have a guide and you do the tapestry, but you don't see what it looks like until you are finished with it. . . . God's will is like that. We see our part, but we do not see the whole thing."

Cardinal McCarrick noted also the significant role that television played in shaping the world's response. Modern media ensure that the world is witness, in real time, to the suffering spawned by natural disasters and war, even in far-flung regions, thus helping to ensure that everyone is aware and affected. The tragedy was rendered all the more poignant by vivid pictures of the beauty of many of the hardest-hit areas—where

BOX 2.1. GOD'S MERCY IN THE AFTERMATH OF THE TSUNAMI

It sometimes takes huge tragedies like the Asian tsunami to prick people into God-awareness. When hearts of flesh turn into hearts of stone, it takes a hammer blow to make any kind of impact. Who knows—the tsunami could well be that hammer blow. Spiritual deafness and blindness have overtaken us. Indulgence dulls our sensitivities, especially our spiritual sensitivity. In this, as in practically all disasters, the majority of the victims are poor. Is it God's will that the poor of Asia, or of any part of the world, live marginalized and utterly vulnerable to the twists and turns in this world of imperfection?

After the tsunami, there was, globally, a great surge of charitable activity, which may reflect something of God's mercy. But human charity should not be equated with God's mercy. God has expressed Her mercy more authentically by giving us the ability to anticipate, avert, or minimize the devastation of so-called natural disasters.

The only way to bear witness to the mercy of God is to address without fear or favor our spiritual calling to stand all that we do on a foundation of justice, compassion, and mercy. Enunciating a caring culture globally must be seen as a minimum agenda in incarnating the mercy of God in this world. God envisaged the whole world as a Garden of Life.

—Swami Agnivesh

upscale tourism has flourished, although surrounded by grinding poverty. As Cardinal McCarrick noted, the waves came ashore about 300 yards, leaving a wasteland in their wake, "but above 300 yards, it was still paradise." The question remains whether life can continue as a playground for the privileged few while surrounded by the poor and suffering.

Thoraya Obaid suggested that the tsunami differed from some other tragedies in that it was "an act of God—not a human-made tragedy, not a tribal war, not an ethnic war. No one has an agenda, economic or political, to fight for or against it. All of this has helped encourage collective responsibility. The question is, can we sustain this collective responsibility and transfer it to human-made crises?"

There were many allusions to the longstanding civil conflicts that have gripped several of the worst affected areas over long years, notably the Tamil-Sinhala conflict in Sri Lanka, the Muslim separatist movement in Aceh province in Indonesia, and the tensions between Buddhist and Muslim communities in southern Thailand. Sulak Sivaraksa suggested one possible beneficial outcome: "In the deep south of Siam, the crisis brought together communities that have long been divided along ethnic lines. We now have the chance to use the destruction to unite Buddhist and Muslim communities despite their deep-seated hostilities and separatist movements."

Cardinal McCarrick similarly noted, with respect to the separatist movements in Aceh: "One would hope for a silver lining here, that people would realize that their conflicts are secondary in light of preserving the whole area."

For many, the outpouring of global support prompted reflection on the meaning and motivation of charity from the perspectives of major faith traditions. In the Jewish tradition, for instance, Maimonides developed the Mishneh Torah code in 1180, in which the highest degree of charity is a gift or loan that makes a needy person self-sufficient. One step below is a gift given so that the recipient knows not from whom he takes. Further down still is a charitable gift given after a needy person requests it. The lowest level of charity is to offer a gift unwillingly. In today's global community, one hopes that the notion of common interest has replaced the notion of charity, but the core of this wisdom is still relevant.

Swami Agnivesh observed, "Human charity may reflect something of God's mercy, but should not be equated with God's mercy. God has expressed Her mercy more authentically by giving us the ability to anticipate human need in the face of natural disasters." However tempting, turning the story of the tsunami into a feel-good story about the generosity of the West—about who gave rather than who suffered—would be wrong. A challenge for the West will be to rise above petty political point scoring and to refrain from turning the story into one whose arc is Christian and Western.

There was unanimous praise and admiration for the work of faith-based groups in providing humanitarian relief, though several present expressly wished to dissociate themselves from reported efforts to mix evangelizing with assistance. Cardinal McCarrick cautioned, albeit gently, "We all love our faiths and love to proclaim the Gospel or the Koran or the Scriptures as we have received them. But when we are there to help, evangelizing should take second place. In some instances, people have been proselytizing more than helping. Let God sort it out."

FROM AID TO COMMUNITY-CENTERED DEVELOPMENT

Aid workers and organizations are planning for a long and complex transition period, moving from emergency work to rebuilding and development. The immediate threats are disease, especially among children; inadequate clean water; and unsanitary living conditions. The challenge is to avoid a doubling (or more) of the death toll as a result of disease.

Rebuilding schools is especially important, both to return children to school and as a vehicle for bringing communities back together. Getting children back to school is among UNICEF's four fundamental steps in any recovery process, along with keeping them alive, caring for separated children, and preventing exploitation. In Aceh alone, some 1,800 teachers died and more than 1,000 schools were washed away. In Sri Lanka, some 150 schools were damaged or destroyed, while another 244 have been converted to house refugees. Remaining schools have lost furniture, equipment, and books. The challenge of rebuilding a sense of security, normalcy, and hope for many children and communities hinges on restoring education systems.

Many people highlighted the urgent need to use funds effectively and transparently, thereby relying on the highest standards of accountability—the more so in light of the great generosity the tsunami disaster has brought forth. Donors and recipient countries have a strong joint responsibility to be conscientious stewards of these funds. Cardinal McCarrick observed that the institutional infrastructure in many of the affected countries is relatively weak, thus creating a special challenge for ensuring that monies are used wisely and effectively. This challenge suggests establishing not only mechanisms to guard against fraud and corruption but also policies and procedures to avoid gaps and duplication. A related concern was that governments, NGOs, and other organizations deliver fully on their pledges. Monsignor Frank Dewane observed, "It is crucial that promises are honored. When financial resources that have been pledged do not appear, not only is it impossible to rebuild the schools, but there is also a much greater cost. We destroy hope."

Master Sheng Yen echoed these sentiments, "Everyone in the disaster areas that we visited strongly believed that all these foreign aid agencies from all over the world are going to disappear after a few months." The global community must focus on the longer-term needs of the affected countries.

How long will this tragedy sustain the world's attention, compassion, and, hence, its financial support? How will the crisis rank among global development priorities? Will pledged financial resources be diverted from other critical programs, such as fighting HIV/AIDS and pursuing global health campaigns against diseases such as malaria, tuberculosis, and polio? The central challenge will be to sustain the generosity generated by a single, visible act of destruction for the more complex task of rehabilitation.

What is the goal of recovery? In the first instance, it should be to reestablish a minimal level of living conditions and the basic elements of a working local economy. But recovery and development should aim at something more ambitious than previous levels of poverty. Recovery efforts should be grounded in community-centered approaches that take full advantage of local resources, culture, and tradition. Hany El Banna underscored that "money should be filtered down to grassroots communities. Projects should be based on the actual needs of the poor, make use of the potential of the people, be easy to implement and appropriate, and benefit the maximum number. Projects should exert an immediate impact on the community; aim to reestablish social units, community forums, and village markets; and encourage creativity."

Equity concerns demand that these efforts favor no group over another. Support for children should include all who live in a community, not just those who lost family or homes. External investment should occur on terms that are advantageous to local communities and should be tailored to their needs. The international business community, foreign direct investment, and governments have sometimes failed on these fronts, and projects should not replicate past errors. Jim Wolfensohn stressed "the importance of understanding the culture and, indeed, the faith of people in these communities and of not trying to remake them in the image of ourselves. Communities cry out for involvement in development; they want to be part of the healing process and to set the agenda for their future as they reconcile with the tragic reality."

CHALLENGES OF PERSPECTIVE

Swami Agnivesh suggested that many "tsunamis" exist around the world. "The only difference is that we have become used to dry-ground tsunamis, whereas the recent Asian tsunami from the sea is a boisterous stranger." Persistent global poverty still presents the world community with its greatest challenge.

Hany El Banna noted, "Poverty is our common enemy. It must be eradicated from our society, not just alleviated." He cited the need for a world order grounded in equality, freedom, partnership, and justice. "Only then can one navigate the rocky shores through which we are now passing and land the ship of humanity in a safe harbor."

Sadly, tragedies must compete for the world's attention. In Africa, more than 29,000 children die every day—and more than 10 million every year—of entirely preventable diseases, lack of clean water, and malnutrition in a world that, in truth, does not know food shortages. During 2004, more than 13,000 people were newly infected with the HIV virus every day, and some 8,500 died each day. More than 15 million children worldwide have lost one or both parents to the disease. The genocide in Rwanda in the mid-1990s took the lives of some 1 million people while the world barely took notice. Thousands of troops have been wounded or killed in the war in Iraq, and hundreds of thousands of Iraqi civilians have died, lost family members, and lost life savings. The tsunami has challenged our core values and stirred us to act. But, like any tragedy, this one raises a fundamental question as to why we react so strongly to some global catastrophes while letting others slip by with so little notice. Dr. Nickson drew a poignant analogy between Sri Lanka and Africa: "I have begun to see the tsunami as a heart attack—acute, very serious, and terrible—but in this case it can be rehabilitated. But the scenario in Central Africa is like a chronic cancer, needing a long-term and holistic approach."

What, then, is the hook that grabs global compassion? Will the tsunami crisis sensitize the world to the plight of the poor? Will it stir more people to ask questions about poverty and about the failure of world leaders and the development community to make progress in eliminating abject poverty? Will it promote higher aid levels to countries that are essentially bankrupt and, therefore, unable to deliver services that rich countries routinely expect governments to provide? Will it motivate developing countries to undertake concerted campaigns against graft and corruption so that they can provide basic services? As Philip O'Brien asked, "How can we use the tsunami crisis and our engagement to sensitize the world about the plight of the world's poor? How do we get people to ask questions about poverty and become advocates for better development assistance and corporate social responsibility? How do we get them to engage in a dialogue about how we can get rid of abject poverty?"

CHALLENGES OF FAITH

Rowan Williams, Archbishop of Canterbury, wrote a personal and compelling note on the challenges posed by the tsunami[1]:

> Every single random accidental death is something that should upset a faith bound up with comfort and ready answers. Faced with the paralyzing magnitude of a disaster like this, we naturally feel more deeply outraged—and also more deeply helpless. . . . The question: "How can you believe in a God who permits suffering on this scale?" is, therefore, very much around us at the moment, and it would be surprising if it weren't. . . . The extraordinary fact is that belief has survived such tests again and again. . . . These convictions are terribly assaulted by all those other facts of human experience that seem to point to a completely arbitrary world, but people still feel bound to them, not for comfort or ease, but because they have imposed themselves on the shape of a life and the habits of a heart. . . . This is why the reaction of faith is or should be always one of passionate engagement with the lives that are left, a response that asks not for understanding but for ways of

changing the situation in whatever—perhaps very small—ways that are open to us.

Each faith has its own means of coping with tragedy, of focusing on the living and the future. Catastrophes such as this one test the metal and the resilience of all faiths and all individuals to find their own strength and commitment. Dublin participants expressed a strong consensus on the need to reach beyond one's own faith tradition to realize the goal of broad and sustained interfaith cooperation. As Swami Agnivesh noted, "The moment we talk of God's mercy in the post-tsunami scenario, the question arises: 'Which God? Whose God?' " Perhaps more than any event in recent history, the Asian tsunami has challenged the world to reach across national boundaries, across cultures, and across faiths in search of answers to such fundamental questions.

NOTE

1. Article appearing in the *(London) Daily Telegraph* on January 13, 2005; the Archbishop was represented at Dublin but was not present there.

(l to r) Rev. Alan McCormick, Dr. Patricia Nickson, Thoraya Obaid, Philip O'Brien, Martin Palmer

3

HIV/AIDS
Morality, Ethics, and
Practical Paths

The spiritual authority of the faith community as the conscience of society is the basis of our renewed enthusiasm for reconstructing life-giving values in combating this pandemic. We are a people of hope because our faith is anchored in the fact that we are not alone. As our commitment is connected to the transforming power of the grandeur of God in all creation, we shall change the conditions that produce anguish and death.

—Reverend Sam Kobia

Reverend Kobia's words graphically illustrate how and why the scourge of HIV/AIDS ranks so high among the many challenges with great and largely untapped potential for partnership between the worlds of faith and development. No issue holds greater urgency for millions of people than HIV/AIDS. Faith leaders exert profound influence in communities and households on an array of issues both spiritual and practical. No other institutions have comparable access to communities through well-developed, on-the-ground networks. Faith institutions, especially at the local level, are well grounded in local culture and inspire levels of trust and confidence unmatched by governments and often secular nongovernmental organizations (NGOs). Above all, faith institutions see and live the dramatic human significance of the pandemic, and, with their development partners, they are poised to act in bold new ways.

To address this challenge, the Dublin participants spoke with a strong undercurrent of hope, anticipation, and determination that, with unwavering commitment, they can achieve progress in fighting the disease in all its many facets. Despite the searing challenges presented by the HIV/AIDS pandemic, stronger partnerships across all segments of society—including a prominent role for alliances among faith-based organizations, and between the worlds of faith and development—are the principal avenue for progress.

The challenge of HIV/AIDS figured prominently and poignantly at the Canterbury meeting of faith and development leaders in October 2002. Institutions and individuals engaged there have since pursued new and more intensive avenues for cooperative work. These avenues have included two multicountry workshops for faith institutions involving nineteen African countries (in Addis Ababa in May 2003 and in Accra in January 2004) sponsored by the World Bank, as well as a mosaic of engagements by organizations such as the Community of Sant' Egidio, which is now treating some 20,000 people living with AIDS in Mozambique, Tanzania, and Malawi; Religions for Peace (focused on children); the Anglican Communion; and innumerable other faith institutions.

Other cooperative activities include the design and launch of the World Bank's Treatment Acceleration Project that is aimed at grappling with the practical and moral dimensions of the urgent need to link treatment of HIV/AIDS with prevention, which specifically includes the Sant'Egidio's Mozambique program. Cooperative efforts have also entailed telling the story of Uganda's HIV/AIDS experience at a major Bank-sponsored meeting on poverty in Shanghai in May 2004[1] and engaging in several international meetings of faith activists in Nairobi, Bangkok, Barcelona, and a first meeting of faith leaders on HIV/AIDS in New Delhi in December 2004. The World Council of Churches convened a meeting in January 2005 to assess the success of faith institutions in gaining access to funding for HIV/AIDS programs, which highlighted the accelerating number of initiatives under way and the strong impetus to act in concert and to find common cause. Of course, the most important activities are the myriad faith-led programs that have a direct effect on people and communities living with HIV/AIDS.

The discussion of HIV/AIDS in Dublin built on this rich lode of experience and dialogue. Several themes permeated the discussion: questions concerning gender, children, and accessible treatment, including antiretroviral drugs, were founded on the concept of a rights-driven approach. Participants explored the implications of the ABC model of prevention, which entails Abstinence, Being faithful, and responsible use of Condoms; the balance between prevention and treatment; and how best to combat stigma and discrimination. Underlying these explorations was a wish to define ways to strengthen faith-development partnerships so that they would have a much broader impact and could be more effective.

DIMENSIONS OF THE CRISIS

The close of 2004 saw some 40 million people around the world who are HIV-positive or afflicted with full-blown AIDS. More than half are women, and some 2.2 million are children. More than 95 percent of people living with HIV/AIDS live in developing countries. Some 5 million—or 12.5 percent—contracted the disease during 2004; the majority were less than 25 years of age. More than 3 million people died of AIDS-related causes during the year. The battle against HIV/AIDS is clearly still raging.[2]

Reverend Samuel Kobia implored his fellow participants, with some urgency, to see the human tragedy behind these numbing statistics. "When you personally lose, not just a loved one, but a whole community of friends and relatives, then your perspective on HIV and AIDS goes through a radical transformation. This is what is happening to us in sub-Saharan Africa, where communities, families, and individuals are helpless as they watch their own sons and daughters bound in hopelessness without medication or preventive facilities to combat the spread of HIV and AIDS. The fact that the old are burying the young—grandmothers are becoming mothers, and children are becoming heads of households—directly affects the cultural and spiritual integrity of ancestral memory."

The face of HIV/AIDS is changing, inexorably and starkly. As Thoraya Obaid noted, "The pandemic is no longer restricted to high-risk groups. It is not only drug injecting. It is not only sex workers. It is not just same-sex relations. It has hit the poor and the marginalized. And the ethical question here is, what do we do in terms of prevention?" The face of

HIV/AIDS is becoming increasingly female and youthful. Rates in sub-Saharan Africa are beginning to stabilize, but that simply means that the number of deaths about equals the number of new infections—hardly cause for complacency. This region is home to more than 25 million infected people—some two-thirds of all cases in the world and, equally striking, some three-quarters of the women worldwide with the disease.[3]

HIV/AIDS has never respected national boundaries. Today, worrisome projections show rapid escalation in regions other than Africa. While the number of people living with HIV is rising throughout the world, the steepest increases are occurring in East Asia, Eastern Europe, and Central Asia. In these flashpoint areas, the main vector of transmission is shifting toward injection drug use, which raises a host of legal issues as well as concerns about how to deliver messages on preventing the disease and combating stigma. At-risk populations are clearly not segregated, as growing prevalence among commercial sex workers—and their clients—inevitably spills over into other segments of society.

As HIV/AIDS continues to wreak havoc on individuals, families, communities, and whole countries, there was a powerful consensus at Dublin that fighting the HIV/AIDS pandemic with all possible resources is the shared responsibility of the world community and especially faith communities, given their deep concerns for justice, equity, and human dignity. And, indeed, faith-based organizations are deeply involved in every area of intervention: prevention, home-based care, orphan care, hospitals, and, increasingly, treatment, including antiretroviral drug therapy. Faith groups provide counseling and family support, including for "aging orphans"—grannies and aunties who, rather than being looked after in their old age by their children, have instead become the sole caregivers for their orphaned grandchildren.

The impact of HIV/AIDS differs vastly depending on whether the infected person is a woman, child, or man, and on where that person lives on the planet. The inequities surrounding this disease partly reflect financial inequalities, which in some respects are fairly straightforward. However, the inequities also reflect deep-seated historical developmental failures and cultural traditions and practices and are, therefore, profoundly complex. Reverend Kobia pointed to one often-overlooked aspect: namely that, at least in Africa, Christian missionary activities sometimes displaced or distorted local traditional religious practices as conveyors of morals and values. In some communities, this approach has left gaps in the social fabric, which exerts critical influence on the spread of HIV/AIDS; the very survival of communities depends on appreciating these patterns and taking them into account. He added, "Traditional sex education and the relationship between different members of the community were informed, shaped, and regulated by the traditional religions. In destroying this intricate relationship between the life of the community and its indigenous religion, the churches considerably weakened the communities and undermined the social fabric."

Ethical questions abound around prevention, which is far more cost-effective (and far more humane) than relying on treatment. Faith communities commonly hold strong views and are, thus, key players in defining national and community approaches to prevention. Thoraya Obaid observed, "Prevention is still a moral and ethical question, and that is one area where faith-based organizations should be able to get together and decide what their position is, since it is the first front in the fight against HIV/AIDS." The ABC model—pioneered most successfully in Uganda—advocates **A**bstinence outside of marriage, **B**eing faithful within marriage, and responsible use of **C**ondoms. Not too long ago, many development organizations viewed condoms, if not as a panacea against the spread of HIV/AIDS, as perhaps the major element. However, it is now widely accepted that behavioral change is also a vital component in an overall, holistic HIV/AIDS strategy. There are still many questions about the relative efficacy of various prevention measures. The major finding of experience on the ground, in different communities, is the need for a range of interventions within the full gamut of possible options involving prevention, care, and treatment—against the backdrop of a rapidly changing pandemic and rapidly changing information and practical options for action (notably changing regimes and prices for medications and increasing emphasis on alternative tools like improved female condoms).

Among the more contentious issues relating to preventing HIV/AIDS has been the position of some faiths, most notably Catholicism, on the use of condoms. In this regard, Father Dominique Peccoud underscored that neither the Pope nor the Holy See had ever addressed condom issues, leaving local bishops to formulate their own positions. Father Peccoud quoted Cardinal Lozano Barragan as asserting that condom use could be justified in some circumstances. "The doctrine of the Catholic Church is very clear. To defend one's life against an aggressor, one can kill. So a wife whose husband is infected with HIV/AIDS and who insists on marital relations and might, therefore, pass on the virus to her, which would kill her, can defend her own life by using a condom." Similar examples of changing paradigms can be found within Muslim communities, such as in Uganda and Senegal.

THE CENTRAL ROLE OF WOMEN'S ROLES AND RIGHTS

Gender inequalities are helping to power the spread of HIV around the world. This concern was widely shared among the Dublin participants. Women are biologically, epidemiologically, and socioeconomically more vulnerable to HIV/AIDS. Women and girls represent just over half of all infected people, and their share has been growing steadily over the years. The global figure masks vast disparities among subregions and countries. In sub-Saharan Africa, adult women are 1.3 times more likely to be HIV-positive than men; young women 15–24 years of age are three times as likely as young men of that age to be HIV-positive. In other regions, women still represent less than half of HIV cases, but their percentage is steadily rising. In Russia, for example, women accounted for 24 percent of those diagnosed as HIV-positive in 2001; by 2003, that figure had jumped to 38 percent.[4]

Even in the industrialized world of North America and Western Europe, HIV infections are growing fastest among poor and marginalized women, including minorities, immigrants, and refugees. African American and Hispanic women, for example, represent less than 25 percent of women in the United States but accounted for an astonishing 80 percent of new AIDS cases by 2000.[5] Noting that "HIV/AIDS has a woman's face," Thoraya Obaid suggested that this surge poses a crucial and complex ethical questions regarding the role of women and their access and right to health services, including reproductive health care.

Prevention and education campaigns throughout the world have seldom taken adequate account of gender inequalities and cultural norms, too often assuming an idealized world where women and girls can make free and unencumbered choices with respect to safe sex. The most common route of HIV transmission among women is heterosexual sex, and most infected women have contracted the virus through long-term, monogamous relationships. A rapidly rising share of HIV-positive women aged 15–24 are married. However, the assumption that they are not subject to a high degree of sexual coercion would be fanciful, because women risk infection by partners who have extramarital sexual relations.

Admonitions to young women to abstain from sexual activity until marriage—and then to remain faithful within that relationship—have, therefore, often resulted in a cruel irony. Women may be more at risk once they marry, for at least two reasons. First, a young single woman may have more power to assert herself and negotiate safe sexual practices. Once married, she is much more at the mercy of her husband, who may be likely to engage in extramarital sexual relations—behavior that she is unlikely to influence. Thoraya Obaid issued a strong recommendation: "One thing faith-based people can do right now is to stand in churches, mosques, and temples and advocate for the respect and honor of women—not just as mothers but as keepers of the family, producers in the economy, peace builders, and citizens—to ensure that their bodily integrity is honored and that they have the right to say no if their husbands are infected or are not committed to practicing safe sex."

In many parts of the world, young women—often teenaged or younger—marry much older men, who have wider sexual experience and are, thus, more likely to have been exposed to the virus. In countries where arranged marriage is still the norm, knowledge of sexual practices and sexually transmitted diseases is rare among young women and girls. This lack of knowledge magnifies their risk of infection. A recent UNAIDS survey revealed that in countries as wide-ranging as Cameroon, Lesotho, Mali, Moldova, Senegal, Ukraine, Uzbekistan, and Vietnam, the vast majority of young women aged 15–24 years could not name three means of preventing HIV/AIDS.[6] In Uttar Pradesh, India, 71 percent of married women—all of whom had married before puberty—had no knowledge of sex or sexuality when they began cohabiting with their husbands.

Where women's situation is characterized by poverty, limited education and income potential, and lack of access to resources, sexual favors may be one of the few "assets" poor women possess. Older men may provide financial support to a girl's family to help pay for groceries, school fees, and health care. The African "sugar daddy" is an all-too-familiar icon that locks girls—and sometimes their families—into cycles of dependence that can greatly increase girls' risk of HIV infection. An important physiological fact is that the lining of a girl's womb is not yet fully developed and may, therefore, be more susceptible to infection. Indeed, in Southern Africa, girls often become infected virtually as soon as they become sexually active.

Sexual violence affects women everywhere in the world. Fear of violence may prevent women from trying to negotiate safe sex. The effects of physical abuse—shame, poor self-esteem, isolation, fear of abandonment—may prevent women from seeking information and help. Violence can be even more damaging when it involves the transmission, sometimes deliberate, of HIV. A new and alarming phenomenon over the past decade has been the use of HIV as a weapon of war. Conflict areas such as Rwanda and Kosovo have reported that thousands of women have been raped—even purposely infected with HIV—as part of a campaign of ethnic cleansing. Thoraya Obaid reported that one-third of the women raped during the Rwandan struggle are now dying of AIDS. Father Peccoud gave a further example, noting that, in the Congo, soldiers infected with the virus have been sent to violate women, thereby infecting them and killing off large numbers of the population without firing a bullet. Counseling generally focuses on the risk of transmitting HIV infection to the child—certainly important, but often ignoring the needs of women themselves. Since sexual coercion puts many women at risk of HIV infection, they need prevention methods they can use without men's knowledge or permission—and without fear of reprisal.

Sex and sexuality lie at the heart of many social and psychological aspects of the epidemic as well. A recent UNAIDS report aptly captures the issue:

> Sex is entangled in people's need to seek and express trust, in their search for status and self-esteem, and in their efforts to escape loneliness and relieve boredom. Research in South Africa, for example, indicates that in the context of widespread impoverishment and high unemployment (as well as the absence of affordable recreation), sexual relationships often serve as

opportunities for enhancing self-esteem and peer status and relieving bore-dom. What makes these quests dangerous for so many women is that they are played out not only in areas where HIV has a firm foothold, but in cir-cumstances marked by glaring gender inequality—where men tend to hold the upper hand, and where social norms and legal frameworks often brace that hand.[7]

Clearly, efforts to reduce infection rates among young women and girls must take such realities into account if they are to have any chance of suc-ceeding. This passage also reinforces the need to advocate for a comprehen-sive agenda of women's rights to education, health care, and resources—in the context of human rights.

Basic disparities abound in women's ability to gain access to quality health care. Evidence has long suggested that HIV progresses more rapidly in women than in men. In part, this situation reflects women's unequal access to care and treatment compared with men who have the same severity of disease. Poverty and lack of access to resources and a social safety net are among the biggest barriers, while competition for women's time in the form of work and family responsibilities also limit access to care. Such obstacles need more study, but one obvious avenue is to strengthen reproductive health facilities. Dublin participants also under-scored the need to integrate HIV/AIDS services within the primary health care system, family planning services, and reproductive health institu-tions. Integrating counseling and referral systems for HIV/AIDS with fam-ily planning services could offer some protection against the fear of social censure among HIV-positive women.

Research on HIV/AIDS has focused largely on men. The barriers that women face in gaining access to health care affect their ability to partici-pate in studies, even in developed countries. As a result, much less is known about the progression of the disease in women, their responses to antiretroviral medication, and its side effects. One concern relates to con-nections between estrogen and male-female differences viral loads and CD4 cell counts. The need for more research on the care and treatment of women living with HIV/AIDS is urgent. Mary Robinson pointed to the need for microbicides that could prevent sexually transmitted diseases, including HIV infection, and for further development of and wider access to female condoms.

THE TRAGEDY OF CHILDREN AND YOUTH

When childhood is lost for so many children, our shared future is compromised.

—Mary Robinson

The HIV/AIDS pandemic has exerted an especially devastating impact on the world's children. Thoraya Obaid noted that more than half of new infections fall within the 15–24 age cohort. She posed the central question of whether these youth have adequate access to educational materials on HIV/AIDS, counseling and referral services, reproductive health services, and treatment.

A patchwork of evidence—including studies by Religions for Peace—underscores the critical importance of faith institutions in the daily struggle to care for orphans in HIV/AIDS-affected communities. Some 2.2 million children under the age of 15 are infected with HIV, and millions more are affected by the 38 million adults afflicted with the disease. Some 15 million orphans have lost one or both parents to AIDS.[8] In 1990, less than 1 million children in Africa had lost one or both parents to HIV/AIDS. By 2001, that number had ballooned to 11 million, and it is projected to rise to 20 million by 2010. Equally alarming has been the rising incidence of children assuming the role of caregivers, child-headed households, street children, school dropout rates, and juvenile delinquency. The lives of children affected by HIV/AIDS are marked by a particular brand of stigma, discrimination, exclusion, abandonment, institutionalization, and exploitation. Even if the number of new HIV infections were somehow to drop to zero, the need to address the panoply of concerns around children affected and infected with the virus would continue for decades.

The impact of HIV/AIDS on children not only jeopardizes their well-being and their rights. It also compromises a country's overall development prospects. In the words of Reverend Kobia, "Children carry the banner of hope and compassion that transcends the existential anguish brought about by the HIV and AIDS pandemic. By investing in their education, we are investing in their resilience against the dilemmas facing the continent, which now must be transformed into opportunities for a new and promising future."

BOX 3.1.
LETTER TO HIV/AIDS CHILDREN IN AFRICA

To Our Dear Children Impacted by HIV/AIDS,

You are persons of incalculable worth and dignity. You are beautiful to us and we love you. You have suffered too much because of HIV/AIDS. Some of you have lost your beloved parents or other members of your family. Some of you are sick. Some of you have felt forgotten, alone, and frightened in a world where no one seems to care. Worse, all of you have been made to feel ashamed of your suffering if it was caused by HIV/AIDS. This is not right. Our religions teach us that you should not suffer alone and that you should not be made to feel ashamed.

We are asking all religious people in Africa to be your family. You are to be known, helped, and loved as part of this family. Our churches, mosques, and temples are also your homes. Let them become places of refuge, rest, and help for you. We will work to make sure that people treat you fairly and that you have the chance to go to school, make friends, and be healthy. We ask that you hold on to hope. Never give up on your life. Take our hands, and we will help you to walk with courage into the future, a future with the joy and love you deserve. You are ours. We love you.

—Letter from 200 African Religious Leaders
to Children Affected by HIV/AIDS

The impacts of HIV/AIDS on families and children include the following:

- Fragmented households, as orphans and elderly people from one family can seldom be absorbed into a single household.
- More child labor through the exploitation of orphans, as households struggle to cope with the financial burdens of HIV.
- Wife inheritance.

- Property dispossession upon the death of the male head of household.
- Higher risk of women and girls forced into commercial sex to generate income for household survival.
- Early marriage and pregnancies.
- Higher school dropout rates and more street children, often leading to juvenile delinquency and higher crime rates.

Experience confirms that foster or community-based care of orphans is far preferable to institutional care. Orphanages can provide food, clothing, and education, and some are outstanding beacons of care and compassion. Nonetheless, institutions rarely meet children's needs for emotional and psychological support and generally separate them from peer groups in the community, which can lead to stigma and discrimination.[9] The great majority of orphans in sub-Saharan Africa have been taken in by extended families, which have historically formed an intricate and resilient social security system that is quick to respond to crises. Children in such settings generally receive better care, including access to education and nutrition; are responsible for fewer household chores; and suffer less stigma and discrimination. These systems are quickly being strained to the breaking point, however, as the number of children expands beyond a given household's capacity to cope, thus deepening poverty and deprivation. Reverend Kobia observed that "Africa is known and is congratulated for being community-based, and for having extended families. But we have reached the time when extended families have been extended to the limit."

Non–family-based community care for orphaned children is still seen as preferable to institutional care, although it does carry risks of subjecting them to sexual and physical abuse and unfair labor practices. In either community- or family-based care, however, the resources available per child shrink—as does the care and attention given to individual children, who are often traumatized by the recent loss of one or both parents—as the number of children grows. These forms of care may also sometimes require separating siblings, causing further trauma and sense of exclusion.

The Dublin participants shared their concerns about the growing incidence of child-headed households and its complex and sometimes unclear implications. The appropriateness of child-headed households as a legitimate form of child care sparked much debate. Maintaining and supporting such households can allow siblings to remain together, give them a greater chance of retaining the family home and other assets, and avert the necessity of placing them in foster or institutional care. But life in households headed by young children clearly puts tremendous strain on the child head, and it entails immature parenting and socializing, safety concerns, much greater difficulty in keeping the children in school (and succeeding there), limited income capacity, and vulnerability to exploitation and abuse. Some countries, such as South Africa, are considering various forms of support and protection for child-headed households, even while acknowledging that they are not the best option.

Children who lack parental care are especially vulnerable across the board. Unprotected living conditions foster low self-esteem, poor socialization skills, lack of education and vocational skills, and a tendency toward crime, all of which increase the likelihood of risky behavior, as well as abuse. Girls may feel forced into transactional sex to survive. Stigma is ever-present.

Against this background, far too little attention has focused on HIV/AIDS issues around children and youth—with international and national responses remarkably inadequate. Few countries have identified youth-specific issues or programs in their overall HIV/AIDS strategies, objectives, and programs. Few countries have dedicated lines within their HIV/AIDS budgets for youth programs, and few track resources by either age or gender. Even in a country such as Uganda, with a recognized, widely dispersed network of child care, some estimates indicate that less than 10 percent of AIDS orphans are receiving care.[10] Few countries, donor organizations, or even civil society groups monitor funding for children and youth, so little to no learning occurs in how to design better programs.

Progress in pharmacological responses for adults living with AIDS has not been matched by similar efforts to treat children. For example, co-trimoxizole is an antibiotic that has shown promising results in postponing the progression of AIDS symptoms and prolonging life. It costs about $10 per person per year. Health workers in many developing countries are familiar with the drug, having used it to treat pneumonia and malaria. Yet while it holds great promise, little research is being done on using the drug to treat pediatric HIV/AIDS, and it is not widely available for such use. Clearly, this is an area for immediate study.

Critical knowledge gaps confront a host of care and treatment issues around children and youth. Diagnostic and treatment protocols for infants under 18 months of age are largely unavailable, partly because they are too expensive. Too little is known about proper dosing levels and toxicity and other side effects in treating children with antiretroviral drugs. Programs that help prevent mother-to-child transmission of HIV are seldom linked to other antiretroviral care and treatment programs.

Much stronger advocacy on the part of governments, international agencies, and civil society groups, including faith communities, is urgently needed to ensure that the losses of the current generation are not perpetuated into the next.

EXPANDING ACCESS TO TREATMENT

Justice means responsibility, but it also means rights. The dialogue on the rights of poor people to receive assistance is urgent and important.
—Thoraya Obaid

The issue of access to treatment for HIV/AIDS presents a complex and critical set of concerns for both faith and development communities. Many Dublin participants voiced the concern that access to AIDS drugs is "upside down." The drugs are where the disease is not, and the disease is where the drugs are not, and too often commercial interests preempt human suffering. While AIDS mortality has dropped precipitously in affluent countries as a result of widespread access to lifesaving antiretroviral drugs (ARVs), the situation in poor developing countries is far different. As Reverend Kobia noted, "The availability of antiretroviral therapy has partly changed the perception of the deadly character of the HIV infection for those who can afford to pay. For them, the close link between HIV and AIDS is decoupled, while for the many others with no access to ARVs, the HIV infection will surely develop into AIDS." A worldwide alliance of faith-based groups could lobby government and the private sector for ethically based access to lifesaving drugs. This was the strong consensus of those who met at Dublin.

Some 700,000 people worldwide were receiving ARV treatment in early 2005. That number reflects a sizeable increase from the 300,000 of two years ago but still represents a small fraction of the global need. Against this background, the feasibility of meeting the target of 3 million persons receiving ARVs by 2005—the 3 × 5 initiative of the World Health Organization (WHO)—is called into some doubt. Only the elite and the wealthy in most developing countries have access to ARVs. Even palliative care, which is based on the best community-based, faith-based, or home-based models, is woefully inadequate, with the result that these efforts often amount to little more than hospice care, without even basic medicines to relieve suffering.

Without in any way diminishing the urgent need for more and more effective prevention programs, acknowledgment is growing—on moral, ethical, and practical grounds—that the world simply cannot ignore the need to offer a higher standard of care to the 40 million people living with HIV/AIDS. As Reverend Ted Karpf noted, people living with AIDS in India, Nigeria, and South Africa represent some 40 percent of worldwide demand, and the potential devastation from the disease remains imminent for these and many other countries. Reverend Kobia argued forcefully that access to lifesaving drugs is not only a medical issue but also a global political concern requiring a global political response, and that this is an area where faith communities have a key role to play in shaping future approaches and policy.

The pressing political issues related to prices and patents cause great concern for leaders from development institutions, faith communities, and business, and there was a consensus that an urgent action dialogue is needed here. "Drug prices and patents expose the structural link between inequality and unjust distribution of power," Reverend Kobia asserted. While human rights overall are far more clearly on the global agenda today than in the past—with widening recognition of their practical import—the idea that there is a basic right to access to social services, including, for example, drugs for care, is still far from any reality.

The prices of ARVs vary wildly from country to country, from as much as $15,000 annually in Europe and the United States for branded drugs to as little as $130–$150 annually in developing countries, reflecting recent price declines of branded drugs and increased availability of generic varieties. The Clinton Foundation has helped to negotiate down the cost of branded drugs for a number of countries in Africa. The world of drug prices has, thus, changed fundamentally, but the problems of access, nonetheless, remain daunting. The stark reality is that for most people suffering or dying from AIDS today, especially those in developing countries, there is little prospect that they will be able to obtain or afford ARVs. As many noted, even vastly reduced prices pose a challenge for many African countries where annual per capita health expenditures vastly exceed the cost of treatment. Philip O'Brien set out an objective: "We need to create an environment in which treatment can be not just where the disease is not, but where the disease is."

Still, widespread drug treatment in resource-poor settings—once seemingly a utopian idea—is receiving much greater attention. Earlier concerns that widespread provision of ARVs in Africa would lead to antiretroviral anarchy, because health care systems are so weak, are gradually yielding to some hope grounded in promising models of successful ARV programs—even in very poor communities—based on careful planning and implementation, with protocols which fall within WHO guidelines. The challenge is to devise sustainable programs for people living with both AIDS and poverty.

Experience shows ever more clearly how prevention and treatment are intricately linked. Dr. Patricia Nickson pointed to a vicious cycle where lack of treatment discourages people from seeking testing and prompts them to continue to engage in unhealthy living practices. The link between prevention and treatment is grounded in technical, financial, medical, and social issues, but it has particular resonance when viewed from an ethical perspective. Earlier arguments ran that, in poor countries and communities, the best strategy was to focus solely on prevention, primarily because the poor could not afford treatment. And, indeed, prevention remains at the heart of any effort to halt HIV/AIDS. However, access to lifesaving medication motivates people to undergo voluntary testing and to take measures to prevent the spread of their disease. The choice between prevention and treatment is a false one. As one speaker noted, one cannot wait for people to get sick and then expect to give them medicines for the rest of their lives, nor can one work only on preventive interventions that entail behavioral changes. People's behavior does change; ample country-based evidence supports this. But lives are lost in the interim. Both tracks are needed and closely linked.

Another central priority, which involves virtually all sectors of society, is the urgent need to strengthen the health care infrastructure. Provision of antiretrovirals is only one component of a comprehensive health care program. Significant expansion of treatment calls into question whether many countries now have the capacity to provide monitoring and diagnostic facilities and to train their health-sector staffs, and whether they can accomplish these two tasks within a reasonable time frame. A number of alternative models that entail public, private, and community-based partnerships are now being tested for their effectiveness in specific African environments.

More focus is also needed on treatment complementary to drug therapy. Mario Giro recounted the experience of the Community of Sant'Egidio in Malawi, Mozambique, and Tanzania, where a holistic program that stresses good nutrition and treatment of physical, mental, and spiritual life works best. Treating opportunistic infections can prolong life and extend the period before which drug therapy is appropriate. Programs need to include such complementary components to both extend lives and vastly improve their quality.

Once drugs become available, the next major issue that presents itself is adherence. Cultural and practical influences on adherence abound, and treatment programs need to take them into account. Reverend Karpf observed that the recent availability of simplified doses—three drugs in one tablet taken twice daily—should address a number of adherence challenges. In Uganda, community-level models support adherence with "buddy systems" and report cards ensuring that people take their medications on time. Partners in Health, whose work in HIV/AIDS is centered mainly in Haiti, ensures that people comply with drug treatments for tuberculosis by taking medicines directly to people who need them. This kind of vigilance, while seemingly impractical, might indeed be practical in some circumstances with dedicated support.

Some troubling ethical questions cannot be avoided, especially where resources are scarce. Should certain categories of people, such as medical professionals and teachers, have privileged access to treatment? Or should advocates work for an equitable treatment program for all or work on a "first-come, first-served" basis? Governments need to develop and refine policies to address these questions, and international leaders need to take a stand in some instances. Overall, treatment coverage should be as equitable and comprehensive as possible, and higher levels of commitment and effort are required to enable governments and other providers to achieve that goal.

In future flashpoint areas—namely, Eastern Europe and the South Asian subcontinent—the vector for transmission of HIV is as or more likely to be injection drug use than sexual contact. Addressing stigma may well be more complicated when HIV-positive people engage in illegal drug use because it involves closer links to crime and criminal networks. This illegality is likely to have implications for efforts to provide treatment, for the degree to which the greater community will support it, and for whether it is tied to policing. Faith communities and leaders can play vital roles in helping construct effective and humane approaches to curbing the spread of HIV through drug use.

However promising, ARV drugs are not the final answer. Most people may well be unable to survive 20 to 50 years without cumulative drug resistance, side effects, and simple weariness, and there are heavy costs involved. Some evidence suggests that economic factors may be making HIV/AIDS a less attractive prospect for drug companies, suggesting the need for public support for further research. (Public agencies, including the National Institutes for Health in the United States, funded much of the initial research on drug treatment for HIV/AIDS.)

The HIV/AIDS pandemic highlights the basic reality that drugs alone will not solve the problem of infectious disease in impoverished nations. Effective treatments for malaria and tuberculosis have been available at reasonable prices for decades in many countries, yet millions still die annually from these diseases. If we have learned anything, it is that public health advances in the developing world require a global commitment to comprehensive health care. Drugs will be needed, but so will efforts to manage side effects, supportive care, diagnostics, clean water, sanitation, and basic nutrition—all areas where faith-based organizations have ample experience. The world can either wring its hands in despair at the overwhelming level of need or acknowledge the complexity of the problem and begin collaborating worldwide to take on the challenge.

STIGMA AND THE ROLE OF FAITH COMMUNITIES

Faith leaders and organizations are not just part of the solution on HIV/AIDS (however important that may be). The Dublin gathering agreed, with great candor, that they are also part of the problem. Despite notable progress, especially among faith leaders and institutions in Africa, stigma is still firmly entrenched. Bishop Gunnar Staalsett challenged faith groups to recognize that "religious communities have to be aware that they are carriers not only of compassion but also of stigma." Others gave specific examples of instances where churches in some African communities do not bury people who have died of AIDS-related symptoms, for fear of "contaminating the soil." There was a report that some faith institutions are still excommunicating people who admit to being infected.

Stigma is closely linked to skewed distribution of power and influence. Hence, the impact on women and children is especially perverse and severe. Reverend Karpf observed that "women can be beaten or killed for their disclosure, and children tragically in too many parts of the world are still seen as expendable, so that the discovery that they are HIV-positive often leads to their brutalization."

Yet, there was also a powerful call to the special role of faith leaders in combating stigma—in breaking down the barriers between "us and them," in the words of one participant. Referring to the World Bank's study *Voices of the Poor,*[11] Bank President Jim Wolfensohn reminded the group how influential faith leaders are in day-to-day issues affecting communities worldwide. In many communities, those leaders inspire higher levels of trust and confidence than any other local institutions and, therefore, have a commensurate potential to combat negative influences such as stigma.

Reverend Kobia noted candidly, "Churches cannot credibly work on HIV and AIDS in partnership with other actors if they do not overcome their own contribution to stigma and discrimination, which have their roots in the ambivalent history of missions and the role of churches in society." Until the link between sin and HIV/AIDS is definitively broken, stigma will continue to haunt and hinder efforts to combat the disease. Even in countries like Uganda, too many churches and mosques have yet to break this link. This area is clearly one for dialogue and outreach.

There are no easy solutions, no silver bullets, to combating stigma. Still, several leaders pointed to a growing number of models that are showing significant scope for addressing the problem. Dignifying people living with AIDS and ensuring that they are at the core of outreach campaigns as both beneficiaries and mentors—firmly engaged as part of the solution—are important. Also essential is supporting networks of people living with AIDS and champions such as Canon Gideon Byamugisha, the Anglican priest who is openly living with AIDS in Uganda. Reverend William Lesher underscored the need for training within religious communities in leadership skills and overall education on HIV and AIDS— both instrumental in combating stigma.

Reverend Kobia highlighted a promising initiative, which was launched by a number of NGOs, to formulate a code of conduct that includes practical guidelines on addressing stigma. The code aims to empower people living with AIDS to understand their rights and to respond to discrimination; to establish mechanisms for monitoring stigma; to educate communities against stigma; and to foster partnerships among human rights institutions, legal services, and other organizations to address stigma.[12]

PARTNERSHIPS AS A FOUNDATION FOR SUCCESS

The world has seen all too few examples of country-level success in addressing the HIV/AIDS pandemic. However, the three most commonly cited "success stories"—Senegal, Thailand, and Uganda—reveal one common thread despite very different social and religious landscapes: vigorous partnerships across every segment of society. Such partnerships begin with courageous political leadership, which paves the way for the active engagement of every sector of society. Each success story has included a prominent role for faith communities in shaping policies and strategies— and in becoming significant providers of care, counseling, and treatment.

The vital role of partnerships emerged as a central theme and a central imperative at Dublin, with repeated challenges to examine critically what more individuals and organizations can do. As Lord George Carey asked, "The HIV/AIDS pandemic is a remorseless tsunami. . . . What are the specific challenges facing faith communities? What more ought we be doing?"

Thoraya Obaid pointed to the need for collaboration among faith groups even in the face of different perspectives: "We as a network can reach agreement on where each one lies on this continuum of assistance, where we can meet, and where we differ. And where we differ, how can we use our comparative advantages?" One speaker suggested that the River Blindness (Onchocerciasis) Program—which has involved multiple donors, NGOs, and faith-based groups—might hold valuable lessons in fighting HIV/AIDS.[13]

On a practical level, the group stressed that despite significant progress in building global partnerships and mobilizing incremental resources, significant roadblocks in linking those with local conditions and capacity remain. Reverend Bill Vendley noted "a significant balloon of money at the global level," but cautioned that "it is having a difficult time getting down to local communities that desperately need it." UNICEF and Religions for Peace recently surveyed the activities of some 670 faith-based groups in six African countries in support of AIDS orphans and other vulnerable children.[14] The groups spanned a wide gamut in size and capacity, and, indeed, only about 370 organizations reported back. But the reach of even this partial group was impressive, encompassing some 15,000 volunteers assisting some 150,000 children. Admitting that these organizations "may not always have been pursuing the best interventions, but doing what they could with the resources at hand," Reverend Vendley highlighted the scope of these networks for affecting huge numbers of children across Africa: "We do not have to ask congregations to be other than what they are. We don't have to build a single one of these mosques or churches or temples. They are already there and already staffed." But these local groups have a huge need for added capacity and resources. He added, "The chain is not robust enough. The Council of Imams does have a link with every mosque in the countries, but is it a micro-financing link? Not yet. Could it be an education link? Absolutely."

Many other types of partnerships are possible and needed, pointed out Mary Robinson. Of special importance is the private sector and, there especially, efforts to frame corporate responsibility to include the right to health. Others suggested that developed countries jointly advocate for further reductions in drug prices and form global procurement alliances that are aimed at driving prices down. The clear and daunting challenge for the group, in the wake of the Dublin meeting, is to enhance existing partnerships and to make new avenues for collaboration a reality.

NOTES

1. Lucy Keough, "Conquering 'Slim': Uganda's War on HIV/AIDS," Global Learning Process on Scaling Up Poverty Reduction, Shanghai Conference, May 25–27, 2004.

2. *AIDS Epidemic Update December 2004* (Geneva: UNAIDS).

3. Ibid.

4. Ibid.

5. Ibid.

6. Ibid.

7. Ibid.

8. This figure is from *Children on the Brink 2004*, a report from UNAIDS, UNICEF, and USAID. This document defines orphans as including children under the age of 17; previous reports have defined orphans to include children under the age of 15. http://www.unicef.org/publications/cob_layout 6-013.pdf

9. *Children on the Brink, 2004.*

10. Kalanidhi Subbarao and Diane Coury, *Reaching Out to Africa's Orphans: A Framework for Public Action* (Washington, DC: The World Bank, 2004), xv.

11. Deepa Narayan, Raj Patel, Kai Schafft, Anne Rademacher, and Sarah Kock-Schulte, *Voices of the Poor: Can Anyone Hear Us?* (New York: Oxford University Press, 2000).

12. http://www.ifrc.org/docs/pubs/health/hivaids/NGOCode-about.pdf

13. "Global Partnership to Eliminate Riverblindness," http://www.worldbank.org/afr/gper/.

14. "Study of the Response by Faith-Based Organizations to Orphans and Vulnerable Children," Preliminary Summary Report, World Conference of Religions for Peace and UNICEF, 2004.

Archbishop Diarmuid Martin and Jean-Louis Sarbib

Lorna Gold and Mary Robinson

Voiceless Majorities
Women and Youth

Each faith tradition needs to investigate the factors that isolate women, youth, and the very poor. Midway through my time as Archbishop of Canterbury, a politician asked me, "When you visit places and dignitaries around the world, who speaks for the women and the orphans?" May I suggest that from now on, in all our work, we ask, "Who speaks for the women, the children, and the orphans?"

—Lord George Carey

Women and youth compose about three-quarters of the world's population. Yet they are often virtually without voice, particularly in sociopolitical decisions, either because they are dimly heard or because their views are simply ignored. The result is a wide spectrum of inequities that include harmful traditional practices, violence and sexual abuse, suffering from armed conflict, limited access to reproductive health and basic social services, and stunted economic opportunity. This array of topics was of central concern at the Dublin meeting.

Gender concerns are key to the Millennium Development Goals (MDGs), and their critical importance for family welfare attracted considerable comment at the Canterbury meeting of faith and development leaders in October 2002. Since then, there has been increasing recognition of the links between the social changes accompanying modernization and the especially strong influence they exert on gender roles. However, while participants at Canterbury agreed on the immense importance of gender and the transformative influence that both faith and development institutions can play, significant differences in how to approach the topic were evident. The Dublin participants challenged themselves not only to advance communication on this sensitive front but also to seek common ground for joint action.

Canterbury participants also saw concerns relating to children and youth as fundamental, but there was little specific agreement on how to approach the topic beyond highlighting the glaring need to combat poverty among youth and to expand access to education. Little explicit discussion occurred on how faith institutions and development institutions viewed policies and programs affecting children and youth. The Dublin meeting took place against a backdrop of mounting attention to children and youth among many faith and development organizations, the World Bank in particular. Participants did agree that youth should figure much more prominently across a range of global concerns, including education, employment, child labor practices, HIV/AIDS, orphans and other youth at special risk, globalization, terrorism, and values.

GENDER CHALLENGES

Gender inequities and biases are manifold in the cultures of developing and developed countries alike, from Europe, to Africa, to the United States, to Latin America, to East and South Asia, and to the Middle East. Whether in the home or the workplace—in church, synagogue, temple, or mosque—women have less status and less power to negotiate decisions and to take actions that directly affect their lives. Although they often carry equal or greater responsibility for supporting their families than their male counterparts, they earn less income.

In many countries, traditional roles are evolving rapidly as women become more educated and enter the workforce in greater numbers, and as divorce becomes more available. In other countries, women remain essentially entrenched in traditions that render them subservient, without voice and with poor access to basic resources. Akbar Ahmed noted that "in traditional societies, the role and position of women is at times tragic." Pointing to the experience of Afghanistan, he observed "that in times of upheaval and rapid change, their status can become a catastrophe."

While globalization expands the menu of opportunities for women, their choices remain more constrained than those of men. Many gender-related issues reveal striking commonality across countries, societies, communities, and households, and no one remains unaffected. Because differences between men and women in their personal and professional lives are worth celebrating, the central goal is best framed as *equity* rather than *equality*: fairness and balance in opportunity, access, and status (see box 4.1).[1]

International treaties, charters, and conferences have addressed gender discrimination for decades, notably the 1979 convention on the Elimination of All Forms of Discrimination Against Women, and the Beijing Conference on the Status of Women in the mid-1990s, as well as follow-ups through the decade. Yet despite widespread international support for these efforts, gender inequity remains deeply entrenched. Pointing to countries such as Bangladesh, Indonesia, and Pakistan—all of which have had female heads of government—Akbar Ahmed observed, "There is clearly no dearth of talented, intelligent women, but they can play their part only if given a platform, and that is especially important in traditional societies."

The MDGs provide a framework for judging progress in reducing poverty and improving living standards among the world's poor by 2015. The third goal calls specifically for promoting "gender equality and the empowerment of women as effective ways to combat poverty, hunger, and disease, and to simulate development that is truly sustainable." Indicators to measure progress on this front include the primary school enrollment rates, the literacy rates, the share of women working in non-agricultural jobs, and the proportion of seats in national parliaments held by women. However, because of the fundamental role of women in development, gender issues critically influence all the other MDGs, including reducing poverty, ensuring universal primary education, reducing child mortality, improving maternal health, combating HIV/AIDS and other communicable diseases, sustaining the environment, and developing global partnerships.[2]

Social, cultural, and religious traditions and institutions all contribute to the lesser status and power of women. The multiplicity of these sources of discrimination suggests the need for an inclusive dialogue and broad partnerships. With government and civil society organizations, faith com-

BOX 4.1. FRONT YARDS AND BACK YARDS OF DEVELOPMENT

In my grandmother's day, houses had special spaces for men and women, reflecting the special role of each in family and community life. In the front yard was a raised platform, a place of authority where men gathered to discuss politics and the affairs of the world. Inside the house was a common sitting room for the whole family. Beyond this, the kitchen had a special niche for gods and goddesses. Finally, in the back yard was a special space for the women of the family. Here they grew flowers for the deities and herbs for cooking and healing aches and pains. It was in the back yard that women socialized and came together to help each other.

While the front yard exercised power and authority, the back yard handled social, cultural, and religious concerns. The back yard was known as a source of help, as a base of spirituality and peace, and as a bond that kept the community together.

Almost a century ago, Gandhiji discovered the importance of the back yard when he returned to India from South Africa to embark on his movement. He traveled extensively all over India, by train, bullock cart, and foot, trudging miles over dusty roads. He stopped at the huts of the dispossessed, not to collect abstract knowledge but to gain a deeper understanding of the poor. Gandhi's political and economic movement received major support from women. He often told people that the moral and economic salvation of India rests with women. Because he understood and acknowledged women's greater capacity for suffering, he believed that women could and would stand up for truth and development more effectively.

In the Hindi language, the word for woman is *mahila*, which means "the strong one." We need to acknowledge the strength and spirituality of women as essential in safeguarding peace and promoting sustainable development. The symbols of Gandhi's political and economic fights were centered on women: the choice of salt for the famous Salt March, and his emphasis on the spinning wheel. He held that a country or community in which women are not honored cannot be considered civilized.

Development often seems to have largely ignored the poor and women—the back yard of our countries. There are innumerable instances in India, Africa, and other parts of the world where rural women, illiterate women, and poor women have fought social and moral battles for survival. One striking example is the famous Chipko movement in India, where a handful of women in the hills clung to the trees to save them from the contractor's axe. The commitment of these few back yard women has exerted a profound influence on the movement to protect forests, conserve water, and retain herbal medicines in India, and it has become a powerful political force for conservation. Equally impressive is the famous Self-Employed Women's Association (SEWA) movement, through which poor vegetable and street vendors have fought and won battles for the use of street spaces for their livelihoods. Movements such as Chipko and SEWA have expanded worldwide because back yard women understand these issues, feel them deeply, and have taken the lead to tackle them in poor and developing countries.

Poverty has a woman's face. In many parts of the world, women bear the greatest burden of human deprivation and degradation. We need to hear the voices of the back yard more clearly and loudly if our visions and actions aimed at creating peace, eradicating poverty, and ensuring sustainable development are to succeed. We need to strengthen the voices of the women in the back yard if we wish to solve the problems of equity, poverty, and peace in the world.

—*Kamla Chowdry*[3]

munities can play a vital role in ensuring gender equity. Thoraya Obaid challenged faith leaders to join the effort: "I do not think that religions assign women a lower position, though that may be the practical outcome of lived practices. Yet the essence of all faith is equity and justice, and if we accept that spirit, then women should not be disadvantaged and voiceless. Religious leaders can promote that message so women are no longer voiceless."

Women and Poverty

Women are productive members of every country, community, household, and faith throughout the world. They shoulder multiple responsibilities, from home care and childrearing, to education both secular and religious, to market gardening, to factory assembly lines, to corporate boardrooms. Yet their work is underreported, as well as undervalued; their access to resources and technology is often constrained; and their ability to shape decision making is limited.

In developed and developing countries alike, women generally work longer hours than men and thus suffer from "time poverty." In developing countries, women spend long hours obtaining water and fuel. Ousmane Seck described typical conditions for women in rural Africa:

> Rural women in the African countryside work 17 hours a day just to make sure the family survives. A woman walks 10 or 15 kilometers a day to fetch water. When she is sick or pregnant, she still walks those 15 kilometers. We would like to enable African women from the countryside to find a few hours to do something else. . . . Village projects; small rural holdings; efforts to build capacity, health centers, and hospitals—all these programs concern women. So in assessing these projects, officials should not talk only to local government authorities. Go and listen to the women.

In rural households women often remain subservient to fathers, husbands, and brothers. Women's contribution to household welfare is pronounced yet often valued least. Because of their lower status, women and girls often eat last and are, therefore, more susceptible to hunger and food insecurity. Boosting the share of household income controlled by women is fundamental to improving this situation.

Despite almost universal recognition that female education is the single most effective investment a country can make, most low-income countries report significant gaps in school enrollment and attendance between girls and boys. Even when girls and boys start school at the same rate, girls are much more likely to drop out, because their labor is called for at home or they become pregnant. Low levels of maternal education translate into malnutrition, child mortality, and poor child care. Investing in educating women and girls yields multiple benefits in terms of income, education of present and future generations, and health and nutritional status. Education can empower women and help to bring down the incidence of domestic violence. Because faith communities provide a significant share of education in many developing countries, even beyond their powers of moral suasion, those communities can play a pivotal role in ensuring equitable enrollment for girls.

Akbar Ahmed highlighted the importance of both secular and faith institutions in socializing children, notably in teaching respect between boys and girls. He stressed, though, that education, especially in rural villages, must be relevant to local conditions and comprehensive: "Traditional societies do not necessarily think in the same terms as post-industrial societies. We need to put poverty in the broad context of faith traditions, but interpret it so that the universal elements come to the fore."

Some 150 million children in low- and middle-income countries are malnourished, and 140 million children will remain malnourished by 2020, given current rates of progress. Although women provide a majority of the agricultural labor force and produce more than half the food in many developing countries, they have poor access to land ownership and tenure, credit, and other food-related resources. Lack of land title severely constrains women's access to credit and inhibits sustainable agriculture. New agricultural technologies often ignore the role of women. Expanded access to productive assets and resources for women can have an immediate effect. One estimate suggests that if women's access to agricultural inputs were on a par with men's, agricultural output in sub-Saharan Africa could grow by 20 percent.[4]

Socioeconomic progress in many countries can be linked to efforts to enhance the roles of women. Nambar Enkhbayar described efforts to improve the status of Mongolia's women: "We have adopted a gender initiative program. We have decreased maternal and child mortality rates. We have given school supplies to some poor families and paid their school fees, with the result that enrollment rates are higher among girls than among boys. This is especially evident at the university level."

Women now represent 70 percent of judges, doctors, nurses, and teachers. But the picture is still mixed: "Some 52 percent of unemployed people are women, and the poorest families are those headed by a single mother."

Women and HIV/AIDS

HIV/AIDS is becoming a disease with a feminine countenance (see chapter 3 for more on these issues). Women are disproportionately infected, especially those who are young and poor, in both developing and developed countries. Most prevention efforts take inadequate account of the unequal terms on which most women conduct their lives. Deeply engrained cultural traditions in many developing countries mean that women cannot negotiate safe sexual practices. Ironically, this situation may be especially true for married women, as single women may wield greater influence over such matters.

Women are less educated about sex and sexuality, especially in countries where arranged marriages prior to puberty are common. Women are biologically more disposed to become infected and have lesser access to health services, including reproductive health facilities. Pharmacological research has paid far less attention to women's issues. And when a family suffers disease and death from HIV/AIDS, women—young and old—shoulder the greatest burdens of care. Gender dimensions clearly warrant far greater attention at all levels of the battle against HIV/AIDS, including prevention, care, and treatment, and both development and faith communities belong at the forefront of efforts to realize this goal.

Reproductive Health Rights

"Women live in two separate worlds," observed Thoraya Obaid. "There is my world, where women have access to safe and affordable health, and there is the other world where—and this is stunning—every single minute a woman dies because of pregnancy-related complications. We are talking about providing women with the basic right to live when giving birth." Gaps in reproductive health care account for about one-fifth of the worldwide burden of illness and premature death, and for one-third of illness and death among women of reproductive age.[5] This impact is heavily concentrated in poor countries.

In the decade since the 1994 Cairo International Conference on Population and Development, encouraging progress has improved women's access to family planning and the quality and reach of other reproductive health programs. But HIV/AIDS and other sexually transmitted diseases continue to spread, and high maternal and child mortality, high fertility rates, and deeply entrenched poverty remain widespread. Women's ill health and unplanned births prevent families from escaping poverty. Poor women have far less access to a skilled birth attendant, the most costly element of reproductive health services. Because access to contraceptives is also largely wealth-based, poor women have children at much younger ages and have more children overall than richer women. Poorer countries have higher risks of maternal, infant, and child death. All too common today (despite well-known techniques to prevent these horrors) are unwanted pregnancies that lead to unsafe and illegal abortions, deaths of mothers in childbirth, and deaths of children before they reach their fifth birthday.

The impact on women's health—and, by implication, on their children's health—of poor access to safe and legal family planning and reproductive health services needs urgent attention from every sector of society.

Women in Professions

In industrial countries, women's wages average 77 percent of men's for comparable work; in developing countries, the rate is 73 percent. Only about one-fifth of this gap can be explained by differences in education, work experience, and job requirements. Women remain vastly underrepresented in national and local political assemblies, averaging less than 10 percent of the seats in national parliaments.[6] Women are equally underrepresented in management positions of private companies, and in both the developing and developed world a wage differential persists between men and women.[7] Yet a wide array of evidence points to the benefits that a balanced workforce can bring. As an illustration, connections between gender and corruption have not been decisively investigated, but some evidence suggests that enterprises with greater representation of women at managerial levels are less corrupt.

Women's Legal Standing

In no region of the developing world do women have equal legal, social, and economic rights. Women cannot vote in many countries, and laws restrict women's employment, ownership of productive resources, inheritance rights, and travel. In some countries, women lack equal standing before the law, religious as well as civil. Pointing to the examples of Afghanistan and Iraq, both with recently inaugurated democratic processes, Akbar Ahmed noted the importance of enfranchising women and ensuring that women are part of the political process: "Traditional and tribal elders are out of touch; they don't know what women want."

Violence against Women

Unequal status, income, and access to social and economic resources all contribute to gender-based violence throughout the world. Laws, institutions, and social norms often tolerate—if not condone—such violence. The teachings of Islam and Christianity are profanely distorted worldwide to justify physical and psychological abuse of wives and daughters. "Honor" killings and maimings are the most virulent form of violence against women, in which women are murdered or assaulted for alleged immoral behavior that is thought to reflect on the honor of the husband and family. The United Nations estimates that "honor" killings account for the murder of more than 5,000 women every year, although the actual number could be much higher, with legal systems giving assailants virtual immunity.[8]

Honor killings have reportedly risen markedly in Iraq since the U.S. occupation of that country.[9] The use of rape has also surfaced as a tool of war in a number of recent conflicts. Bride burnings, the sex trade, child sexual abuse, rape, and sexual harassment (in its many different forms) all speak to the abuse of power, with the weak and dispossessed unable to respond. Akbar Ahmed recounted the recent rape by military officials of a female doctor serving in the remote Pakistani province of Baluchistan. The ripple effects of such incidents spread beyond the village to the tribe and then the province, as tribal leaders revert to ancient traditions and "the women disappear. They are already half invisible. No chief will allow his women to be out there, if there is a chance they will become hostages." Such crimes thus arrest the advance and education of women throughout a society.

Other Dimensions of Poverty

Women are affected disproportionately by poverty and its many dimensions, including lack of empowerment, opportunity, capacity, and security. What is more, poverty breeds inequality just as inequality furthers poverty. Compounded by social and cultural traditions that seldom work in women's favor, that vicious circle accounts in large measure for the high shares of women-headed households living in poverty in many developing countries and for their seeming inability to rise above the poverty level.

While women and girls bear the brunt of inequality, the economy and society also ultimately bear the costs. Gender inequities undermine productive labor and efficient allocation of resources at both household and national levels. Evidence is incontrovertible that investment in women and girls has far-reaching benefits for all members of society—women, men, girls, and boys. Enhancing education and employment opportunities for girls and women boosts production, moderates fertility rates, reduces child mortality, and improves health indicators, among other positive effects.

Robust women's associations can make a dramatic impact on the breadth, depth, and effectiveness of public debate about these topics, at both national and international levels. Thoraya Obaid urged faith and development leaders, for their part, not only to include women in decision making but also to legitimize their dignity: "We can't just see women as victims. They are the ones who keep the family and the community together."

SPECIAL CHALLENGES FOR CHILDREN AND YOUTH

Young people clearly are a major force in the world—not only for the future of society but also for the present. Dublin participants saw today's youth as agents of social, economic, and political change; the dialogue revolved around how best to build a constructive dialogue with them. Of

some 6 billion people in the world today, nearly half—some 2.8 billion—
are under the age of 24, while about 1.8 billion are younger than 14. The
cohort of 15- to 24-year-olds accounts for 18 percent of the global population, or 1.1 billion people.[10] In the next 30 years, this cohort of young
people will rise to 2.5 billion.[11]

Young people are growing up in a globalizing world that is reshaping
the transition from one phase of life to the next and redefining relations
between generations. All young people—from whatever country or social
environment—share a common search for identity and independence
that encompasses personal, psychological, social, institutional, and economic factors.

Yet youth are far from a homogenous group. Their opportunities, experiences, and needs reflect their age, gender, ethnicity, social class, household size, access to education and training, disability, and migrant and
refugee status, as well as the stage of development of the countries in which
they live. Some youth have unprecedented access to technology, travel, and
participation in a global market, while others confront poverty, inequality,
and social exclusion. The latter challenges especially affect the 85 percent
of the world's youth who live in the developing world, underscoring how
far youth issues are intertwined with basic questions of social and economic development and present basic questions of equity and inclusion.

Many young people barely eke out a living:

- Some 238 million young people survive on less than $1 per day.
- Some 133 million youth are illiterate.
- Youth account for 41 percent of the world's unemployed. Many more
  survive precariously in the informal economy (legal and illegal).
- Some 6,000 to 7,000 young people are infected every day with HIV/
  AIDS.
- Girls and young women regularly experience violence and discrimina-
  tion and lack access to reproductive health services.
- Some 300,000 youth worldwide are child soldiers, actively participat-
  ing in violence and combat.[12]

Uncertain income can lead to crime, drug use and trafficking, and risky
sexual behavior. These activities have consequences not only for youth
but also for their families, communities, and larger societies.

Values and Dialogue between Generations

All young people face economic and social uncertainty and volatility as they make the transition from adolescence to adulthood . . . Social policies that focus on youth and their specific challenges can prepare them to move from being recipients of care to becoming active contributors to social, political, and economic life. However, too few channels of communication allow youth, outside their immediate family, to make their voices heard and to help shape policies that affect them and their futures. Striking agreement on the depth and importance of this phenomenon emerged during the Dublin discussions.

Participants offered differing perspectives on avenues for intergenerational dialogue on the motivations and values of youth. Ekaterina Genieva expressed a concern shared by several colleagues: that many youth—at least those in Russia—are living in a world of undermined values have little appreciation for the significance of history. They are simply seeking a "normal life."

Other participants did not share this characterization. Lorna Gold, for example, suggested

We need to avoid the temptation to generalize about young people and their values. One generation always assumes that the next is doomed and that it lacks values. Young people today have many values. Young people founded the World Social Forum [the gathering of civil society groups that parallels the Davos economic summit], and they are driving efforts to promote ethical and fair trade practices. Their problem is often with traditional structures, including religious organizations, where they don't feel they have a voice.

Thoraya Obaid commented, "The media, satellites, and the Internet have developed a globalized youth culture that we adults need to understand. We need to build a dialogue between the old and the young so we can support each other. Youth are listening to you, the religious leaders. This is definitely an area where you can help."

Building trust is as crucial to the well-being of youth as is access to education, health services, and employment. Trust is the basic skeleton of society, its institutions, and its expectations. To foster trust, adults must create a world where children and youth are valued and respected—where their voices are heard and their basic needs are guaranteed. As Ekaterina Genieva observed, "Young people need caring and compassion. That is our responsibility if we want to make friends and followers of them."

Education

Education is the single most important factor determining whether young people will lead productive and responsible lives. Yet some 130 million children are not in school, while about 133 million 15- to 24-year-olds are illiterate.[13]

The commitments reflected in the MDGs present a stark challenge in the face of the profound educational inequalities across many countries. In most North American and Western European countries, primary school enrollment is close to or at 100 percent, while secondary enrollment stands at about 90 percent. This figure contrasts with primary school enrollment in the poorest African countries: Angola, 30 percent; Niger, 34 percent; Burkina Faso and Democratic Republic of Congo, 35 percent; Mali, 38 percent; Eritrea and Ethiopia, 46 percent. Secondary enrollment in these countries is only 5–20 percent.[14]

Education helps socialize children, shaping their norms and values. However, in cultures where children's labor is an important household asset, family and communities are seen as the primary agents of learning and socialization, with formal school systems and curricula secondary. This situation is especially true for girls. Ousmane Seck reminded the group of the central importance of families and faith in providing the moral education for shaping today's youth.

Even youth with some access to schooling may not acquire basic literacy skills, the barometer of educational development. Literacy among young people is generally 90 percent or better in the United Nations Development Program's high- and medium–human-development countries. The average literacy rate among young people in low–human-development countries is 64 percent, and the rates for many individual countries are even lower: Burkina Faso, 19 percent; Mali and Niger, 24 percent; Mauritania, 49 percent; Senegal, 52 percent; and Benin, 55 percent.[15]

In the developed world, the factors that hinder access to education—income levels, gender, social background, and ethnicity—are becoming less important, and the gender gap has shrunk considerably. In the developing world, however, indicators of educational inequity still vary widely by gender. In Western Asia, at least half of women 15 years of age and over are illiterate, and girls are underrepresented even at the preschool level, with the situation worst in poor and rural areas. In sub-Saharan Africa and South Asia, minority group membership, rural location, and poverty contribute to wide gender gaps. Similar patterns exist in some East Asian countries as well as in parts of Latin America and the Caribbean.

Employment

Among all the challenges confronting young adults worldwide, employment is by far the most important. It determines not only their standard of living but also, very often, their sense of self. Underemployment and unemployment lock many young people into persistent poverty, job instability, and social exclusion, which together affect social and political stability and even a region's potential for armed conflict. The International Labour Organization (ILO) estimates that 160 million people worldwide are unemployed, with many more subsisting on the economic margins or holding jobs that do not ensure survival. Young people are disproportionately represented in those groups. Nearly 40 percent of those without work are young people; unemployment levels tend to be two to three times higher for this group than for the adult population. In developing countries, the ILO estimates one-third to one-half of 15- to 24-year-olds are unemployed, and young people who are employed may find themselves in low-paying, temporary jobs with few protections.[16]

Youth who enter the workforce with inadequate education, underdeveloped skills, and limited job prospects face the highest risk of long-term unemployment, underemployment, and low-wage employment throughout their working lives, making them more vulnerable to both poverty and social exclusion. The wider social costs of these effects are profound, including more crime and violence, social unrest, and divided societies.

Fauozi Skali warned of the dangerous links between poverty and the susceptibility of youth to extremist groups: "Extremism is feeding on poverty and the large numbers of marginalized youth, who have no jobs and are in dead-end situations. . . . Extremist religious groups are often more present than the state. When there is a natural disaster, a health problem, a social problem, or a need to support the poor, these organizations are sometimes the first on the ground." Partnerships between faith groups and development groups, he suggests, offer the best antidote.

Successful transition from adolescent dependence to adult independence assumes an ability to find gainful employment, which, in turn, assumes a functioning labor market. In countries where the situation of labor is precarious, youth are especially vulnerable. In industrialized countries, flexible workforces and the growing use of part-time and temporary employment have heightened insecurity and risk. In developing countries, a rising number of young people work in the informal economy, where they earn low wages and are often subject to poor and exploitative working conditions. In both developing and developed countries, the population living below nationally defined poverty lines includes large and disproportionate shares of youth.

Young workers can face serious inequities, as they are less able to object to substandard working conditions. In the service industry, many workers consider their jobs temporary, and they are, thus, less likely to band together to demand better wages and working conditions, especially in regions with an oversupply of labor. The growing use of short-term contracts highlights deteriorating conditions in the youth labor market, and young workers are more likely to receive and accept this type of offer.

In all countries, some groups of young people are more susceptible to unemployment than others. Females overall tend to be far more vulnerable than males. While education and vocational skills often provide some protection, young people with advanced degrees in some countries are ironically more likely to experience unemployment—particularly long-term unemployment—as economic stagnation weakens demand for higher-skilled workers. Other factors that make young people more susceptible to unemployment include a lack of basic skills, disabilities, criminal convictions, ethnic minority status, and responsibility for the care of children or other relatives. All these factors fuel the pressures for migration overseas and tensions at home.[17]

Child Labor

In many very poor households, child labor is an essential part of subsistence. Many working children live in a stable and nurturing environment with their parents or are under the protection of a guardian, and those children may benefit from informal education and training and socialization through work. Some 50–70 percent of working children are also studying. However, premature and extensive engagement in work outside the home prevents children from developing intellectually and mentally, impairing their income-earning ability and often their welfare for life.

Some 211 million children aged 5–14—slightly less than one-fifth of the world's children—were engaged in wage-earning economic activity in 2000. About 73 million children under 10 years of age are working. In both the 5–9 and the 10–14 age brackets, boys and girls are equally likely to be engaged in economic activity, but for older children, more boys than girls work.[18]

The Asia-Pacific region has the largest number of child workers in the 5–14 age category, with 127 million. Sub-Saharan Africa and Latin America and the Caribbean follow, with 48 million and 17.4 million child workers, respectively. Developed and transitional countries have the lowest number of child workers, with 2.5 and 2.4 million, respectively. Sub-Saharan Africa has the highest proportion of working children, with one child in three below the age of 15 being economically active. In the Asia-Pacific region and Latin America and the Caribbean, the incidence is 19 percent and 16 percent, respectively, and in the Middle East and North Africa, it is 15 percent.

Child labor rates are generally much higher in rural than in urban areas, with some 90 percent of rural working children engaged in agriculture or similar activities. Their urban counterparts are found mainly in trade and services, with few in manufacturing and construction.[19]

Inequity and injustice become even more apparent with closer examination of these statistics. Some 171 million children aged 5–17 worked in hazardous conditions in 2000; boys outnumbered girls in all age groups.[20] Some 8.4 million children are involved in the worst forms of child exploitation, including trafficking (1.2 million), forced and bonded labor (5.7 million), armed conflict (0.3 million), prostitution and pornography (1.8 million), and illicit activities (0.6 million).[21] Bonded labor tends to concentrate in South Asia and East Asia and is most common in agriculture, domestic help, the sex industry, carpet and textile industries, and quarrying and brick making.

Children in these sectors suffer long-lasting psychosocial, as well as more immediate, consequences. Children in agriculture are more likely to be adversely affected than adults by climatic exposure, heavy work, toxic chemicals, and accidents involving sharpened tools and motorized equipment.[22] Long hours cause fatigue and, thus, accidents. Domestic service workers typically live away from home and routinely work long hours, often in almost total isolation from family and friends, thereby risking serious psychological and social impairment, as well as physical, sexual, and psychological abuse. As an example, child garbage pickers in the Philippines are known to suffer high risk of disease and disability through exposure to lead and mercury, heavy lifting, and the presence of parasites.

Young People's Health Issues

Poor hygiene, risky behavior, poor basic sanitation, and new and emerging diseases combine in a deadly mix that defies classic images of healthy youth. In all countries—whether developing, transitional, or developed—economic hardship, unemployment, sanctions, embargoes, poverty, and inequality often induce or compound disabilities, as well as acute and chronic illnesses, among youth. The cumulative toll on youth of violence, HIV/AIDS, and tuberculosis adds to the heavy incidence of malaria and vaccine-preventable diseases. Worm infections are the greatest cause of disease among 5- to 14-year-olds, while young people who are 15–24 years old represent up to 60 percent of all new HIV infections. Worldwide, 5 percent of all deaths of young people between the ages of 15 and 29 are attributed to alcohol use.[23]

School and other health programs can prevent or significantly reduce the most pervasive health problems among young people, but many lack access to education and health facilities. In Yemen, for example, 50 percent of children from birth to 5 years of age have no access to basic health care, and 46 percent suffer from malnutrition.[24] Many young people lack information on diseases and bodily conditions and functions that would help determine health status. Parents, schools, and media are responsible for educating children about the personal, physical, and social aspects of health, sexuality, and pregnancy, including preventing and managing sexually transmitted diseases. However, those groups often fail to fulfill or abuse their responsibility. Religious leaders and institutions can play an important role in showing individuals, families, and communities how to promote health and provide a healthy and safe environment for children and youth.

Orphans and Other Vulnerable Children

Vulnerability among children is generally defined as conditions that threaten their safety, well-being, and development. Important factors that accentuate children's vulnerability include inadequate care, affection, shelter, education, nutrition, and psychological support.[25] Orphans are particularly vulnerable because they usually lack the emotional and physical maturity to address the psychological trauma associated with parental loss.

Civil unrest and post-conflict situations are today producing countless orphans and displaced children. But the greatest contributor to orphanage today in many parts of the world is HIV/AIDS. In 1990, fewer than 1 million children in Africa had lost at least one parent to HIV/AIDS. By 2003, that number had ballooned to more than 12 million, and it is projected to rise to 20 million by 2010.[26] Equally alarming are growing numbers of children cast in caregiver roles (often in child-headed households), street children, school dropouts, and juvenile delinquents.

HIV/AIDS represents an unprecedented health, economic, and social threat to all youth, who are particularly vulnerable to infection through unprotected sex, drug use, and mother-to-child transmission. Some 2.2 million children under the age of 15 worldwide are infected with HIV. The lives of these children and HIV orphans are marked by a particular brand of stigma, discrimination, exclusion, abandonment, institutionalization, and exploitation. Even if the number of new HIV infections were somehow to drop to zero, the need to address the concerns of children affected by the virus would continue for decades. Civil society groups—

notably faith-based organizations—can help respond to this crisis while reflecting local needs.

Impact of Drug Use on Youth

Drug use and abuse disproportionately affect children and youth. Young people share many of the same motivations as adults who use drugs: they seek to relieve stress, obtain relief, or heighten enjoyment. Young people may have added motivations: heightened tendency to take risks; a desire to establish independence or win peer approval, and to seek excitement; and—often—a sense of invincibility.

Substance abuse is viewed with growing tolerance in some areas, and more prosperous young people may view drug use as a recreational activity. For disadvantaged, vulnerable, marginalized youth, however, drug use is tied to a quest for relief from physical or emotional abuse, neglect, violence, sexual exploitation, and conflict. Although lines between these two worlds often blur, they are fundamentally different. Vulnerable youth, especially street children, often have traumatic or nonexistent family backgrounds that may include parental abuse, forced institutionalization, and a history of "survival sex"—all of which heighten susceptibility to high-risk behavior, including drug use. Once these youth start down the road to drug abuse, they can find stopping much more difficult than can youth with support structures in place.

Prevention and outreach initiatives to address these challenges span a broad spectrum: education, counseling, job creation, access to safe recreation, and community services. These efforts are more likely to succeed if supported by partnerships among public, private, civic, and faith organizations and leaders. The need to promote a safe and secure environment for street youth by meeting their basic needs for food, shelter, clothing, and access to health care is particularly urgent. Programs also need to address the stigma and exclusion that prevent reaching this segment of youth, thereby contributing to the problem.

Impact of Globalization on Youth

Globalization affects youth in special ways and exacerbates many challenges, including inequity. The spectacular economic benefits that globalization offers contrast with often-significant social costs, such as the erosion of social and cultural values and traditions. The globalization process simultaneously universalizes and individualizes—it brings us all closer together yet divides us more sharply. Thoraya Obaid observed, "What we mean when we talk about globalization is that the world has become very small. But we are many worlds at once, many isolated worlds."

Globalization may well exert its most profound impact on youth, because of their vulnerability, their desire to shape their own identities both economic and social, and their tendency to rebel. The idea of globalization—with all its vagaries and uncertainties—sums up the uncertainties and fears of youth at the turn of a new century.

Globalization creates global markets and patterns of consumption, while advertising makes anything seem possible and within reach. Whether a young person lives in the suburbs of Los Angeles or of Johannesburg, the Internet offers the same tantalizing array of consumer products and—equally important—a sense of identity and inclusion. But consumer culture may remain virtual and distant to young people in poorer communities, thereby sharpening social and economic divides. When consumer expectations cannot be met, they provoke a profound sense of inequity, exclusion, frustration, and alienation.

The cultural dominance of the West is incontrovertible. Apart from the worldwide reach of hip-hop and Hollywood culture, Western agencies produce and transmit 90 percent of the world's news and foster cultural norms and practices alien to many countries and societies. Thus, young people—especially those growing up in developing countries—are beset daily by the need to balance local and global influences. The challenge to households, civic groups, and faith communities is how to effectively engage youth groups and leaders in responding to globalization, and shaping cultural norms and practices could determine a society's future.

In closing this session, Lord George Carey challenged the group: "Each faith tradition needs to investigate the factors that isolate women, youth, and the very poor. Midway through my time as Archbishop of Canterbury, a politician asked me, 'When you visit places and dignitaries around the world, who speaks for the women and the orphans?' May I suggest that from now on, in all our work, we ask, 'Who speaks for the women, the children, and the orphans?' "

NOTES

1. While masculine qualities have long been recognized, women's contributions in many spheres are now receiving more attention. One example: business settings seem to benefit from women's team skills.

2. See annex tables 4.1 and 4.2 for county indicators of gender development and for school enrollment.

3. A scholar of Gandhi and member of many development commissions, Kamla Chowdry is a trustee of the World Faiths Development Dialogue; this text was prepared for the Dublin meeting, though illness prevented her from attending in person.

4. *Engendering Development: Through Gender Equality in Rights, Resources, and Voice* (Washington, DC: World Bank and Oxford University Press, A World Bank Policy Research Report, January 2001), 5.

5. *State of World Population 2004* (New York: United Nations Population Fund).

6. *Gender Equality and the Millennium Development Goals* (Washington, DC: World Bank Gender and Development Group, April 2003).

7. Ibid.

8. Chapter 3, "Ending Violence Against Women and Girls," *The State of the World Population 2000* (New York: United Nations Population Fund, 2000).

9. Vivienne Walt, "Marked Women," *Time Magazine,* July 26, 2004.

10. *World Youth Report 2003: The Global Situation of Young People* (Geneva: International Labour Organization, 2003).

11. "Youth, Development, and Peace 2004," Closing Remarks by James D. Wolfensohn at Youth, Development, and Peace 2004 Conference, Sarajevo, September 6, 2004.

12. *World Youth Report 2003: The Global Situation of Young People* (Geneva: International Labour Organization, 2003).

13. Ibid.

14. United Nations Statistics Division, Millennium Indicators Database, 2004. http://millenniumindicators.un.org/unsd/mi/mi_series_results.asp?rowId=5 89.

15. United Nations Statistics Division, Millennium Indicators Database, 2004. http://millenniumindicators.un.org/unsd/mi/mi_series_results.asp?rowId=6 56.

16. *World Youth Report 2003.*

17. Ibid.

18. *Every Child Counts: New Global Estimates on Child Labour* (Geneva: International Labour Organization, April 2002).

19. Ibid.

20. Ibid.

21. Ibid.

22. *Child Labor: Issues and Directions for the World Bank* (Washington, DC: World Bank, 1998).

23. See http://www.who.int/school3Outh_health/en/.

24. "Yemen and the Millennium Development Goals," Middle East and North Africa Working Paper Series, The World Bank, No. 31, March 2003. http://lnweb18.worldbank.org/mna/mena.nsf/Attachments/WP+31/$File/WP-31.pdf.

25. *Reaching Out to Africa's Orphans* (Washington, DC: World Bank 2004).

26. *Children on the Brink 2004* (New York: UNAIDS, UNICEF, and U.S. Agency for International Development, 2004). This document includes orphans under the age of 17; previous reports included orphans under the age of 15.

Chapter 4 Annex Tables

Table 4.1 Indicators of Gender Development

	Human Development Index (HDI),[a] rank in 2002	Gender-related Development Index (GDI),[b] rank in 2002	Female literacy rate (ages 15 and above), UNESCO 2002	Female net primary enrollment ratio (percent),[c] national data/UNESCO 2001/1	Seats in parliament held by women, UNESCO 2002 (percent)	Share of women in non-agricultural workforce (percent), ILO 2003[d]
Developed countries						
United States	8	8	—	93	14	49
United Kingdom	12	9	—	10	17	50
France	16	15	—	100	12	47
Japan	9	12	—	101	10	41
Africa						
Senegal	157	128	30	54	19	—
Niger	176	144	9	28	1.2	—
Malawi	165	134	49	81	9.3	38
Sudan	139	115	49	42	9.7	19
South Africa	119	96	85	90	28	—
Latin America						
Brazil	72	60	87	97	9.1	47
Mexico	53	50	89	102	21	37

Venezuela	68	58	93	93	10	42
Bolivia	114	92	81	94	18	37
Asia						
India	127	103	46	76	9	18
China	94	71	87	93	20	40
Pakistan	142	120	29	—	21	8.7
Cambodia	130	105	59	83	11	53
Middle East						
Jordan	90	76	86	92	7.9	25
Egypt	120	99	44	88	3.6	22
Saudi Arabia	77	72	70	57	0	15

Source: Human Development Report 2004, UNDP.

Note: — no data available.

a. HDI measures achievements in three basic dimensions: life expectancy at birth; adult literacy and enrollment in primary, secondary, and tertiary schools; and GDP per capita in purchasing power parity (U.S. dollars). The HDI offers a powerful alternative to income as a measure of human well-being (Human Development Report 2004, UNDP, p. 137).

b. GDI uses the same indicators as HDI to measure achievements but it also captures inequalities between men and women. The greater the gender disparity in basic human development, the lower a country's GDI relative to its HDI (Human Development Report 2004, UNDP, p. 128).

c. The net enrollment ratio is the ratio of enrolled children to the total population of that age. Net enrollment ratios exceeding 100 percent reflect discrepancies between the two data sets (Human Development Report 2004, UNDP, p. 228).

d. These data are from the United Nations Statistics Division, Millennium Indicators Database.

Table 4.2: Enrollment levels across regions, 2001, UNESCO

	Ratio of girls to boys, primary enrollment	Ratio of girls to boys, secondary enrollment	Ratio of girls to boys, tertiary enrollment
Developed countries			
United States	1.01	0.99	1.35
United Kingdom	1.00	1.25	1.23
France	0.99	1.01	1.27
Japan	1.00	1.01	0.86
Africa			
Senegal	0.91	0.67	—
Niger	0.68	0.65	0.34
Malawi	0.96	0.76	—
Sudan	0.85	0.89*	—
South Africa	0.96	1.09	1.14
Latin America			
Brazil	0.94	1.10	1.29
Mexico	0.99	1.07	0.95
Venezuela	0.98	1.16	1.37
Bolivia	0.99	0.96	—
Asia			
India	0.85	0.74	0.70
China	1.00	0.92*	—
Thailand	0.96	0.95*	1.09
Cambodia	0.89	0.60	0.40
Middle East			
Jordan	1.00	1.02	1.02
Egypt	0.94	0.93	—
Saudi Arabia	0.97	0.89	1.49

Source: United Nations Statistics Division, Millennium Indicators Database, 2004.
Note: * data from 2000.
 — no data available.

Nambar Enkhbayar and HRH Prince Turki Al-Faisal Al-Saud

(l to r) Rabbi David Rosen, Rabbi David Saperstein, Jean-Louis Sarbib, Ousmane Seck, Sahib Jathedar Manjit Singh

CHAPTER 5

Roots of Conflict, Branches of Peace

The international system today is more interdependent than it has ever been in human history. Our ability to exchange ideas and communicate can help us to break down the barriers of geography and politics, and also the barriers of misunderstandings and misinterpretations between each other. We share a mutual concern for peace, for the welfare of our planet and its environment. We all yearn for a life in which we can live peacefully without conflict, working together for future generations.

—Prince Turki Al-Faisal Al-Saud

The cold shadow of September 11, 2001, was close in time and spirit when faith and development leaders met in Canterbury in October 2002. It set challenges of war and peace in sharp relief and posed ancient moral and practical questions about how religion and social change—together and separately—influence instability and social cohesion, conflict and harmony. In the intervening years, the extraordinary array of global sociopolitical challenges and change has spurred intense reflection about these questions.

Even the debates about causes of conflict have proved contentious, in no small measure because religion and conflict are perceived as joined in complex ways, whether in encouraging competition among groups, or accentuating or even sparking tensions. Lord George Carey, introducing the Dublin discussion, cited a recent book title, *Violence in God's Name: Religion in an Age of Conflict,*[1] as a symbol of the deepening exploration of these links. At the same time, the potential and responsibility of faith leaders and institutions for peacemaking has never been posed and explored as intensively. Individual faith leaders and institutions, as well as interfaith and ecumenical institutions, are today focusing sharp attention on the roots of armed conflict and, still more, on paths to peace.

Reflection on the links between development strategies and conflict and stability has similarly intensified within development institutions and the global community. What is the role of economic growth in conflict? How does the use and supply of natural resources affect social stability? How can we resolve the inequality that fuels social tensions within and among nations? What role does poverty play in conflict? Does globalization accentuate tensions, and does social change undermine ancient mechanisms for resolving conflict? How is equity, at global and national levels, related to stability? Keen debates and new initiatives now under way aim to help ensure that, in the light of experience, development efforts take fuller account of potential and actual social tensions and work to build resilient and peaceful societies. Conflict prevention has an even higher priority than conflict resolution and postconflict reconstruction.

Several Dublin participants were directly engaged in working for the exciting recent accords in Sudan—the site of Africa's longest civil war. This opening symbolized the hope that swords can indeed be beaten into plowshares and civic tension turned into dynamic change. Armed conflict, nonetheless, is still the paramount obstacle to progress for many of the world's poorest countries. The Dublin meeting recognized conflict as the deadly enemy of development and efforts to alleviate poverty. Discussion focused on the far-ranging impact of the Palestinian-Israeli conflict; it drew inspiration from the history of Ireland, with its lessons of hope and reminders of the legacy of conflict and fragility of peace. How can practical responses guarantee equity and justice for all sides? Are faith and development leaders, with their shared passion for peace and justice, fully exploiting their will and skill to work together toward a just and lasting peace?

The call for a richer "dialogue among civilizations" has deepened since Canterbury, with many implications and challenges for faith and development leaders, as well as for those from business and the arts. The "war on terror" and conflicts in Iraq, Afghanistan, Darfur, and elsewhere in Africa highlight the critical need to pursue every avenue for dialogue among all faiths, but in particular, Christian and Islamic traditions, with challenges particularly evident in the South Asian subcontinent, East Asia, and the Middle East, but also coming into sharper focus in Europe. These challenges affect every corner of the world.

The Dublin meeting offered an opportunity to take stock of the roles that leaders from different sectors—both individually and collectively—are playing. The Dublin group carries and seeks no mandate for peacemaking or peacekeeping. Other organizations have assumed that mantle: the United Nations, national diplomatic services, Religions for Peace, the United Religions Initiative, the Community of Sant'Egidio, and the growing body of vibrant civil society institutions. Nonetheless, peace is at the core of the mission of the faith and development leaders who met in Dublin. All share an acute awareness of the intricate threads that bind poverty and misery with social exclusion, anger, despair, ancient grudges, lack of hope for a better future, disease, and breakdowns in social order—all of which leave a fertile field for armed conflict.

Thus, the agenda at Dublin centered on reflections on poverty and inequity as causes of violence; on the role of faith groups in peacebuilding and reconciliation; and on how best to combine inspiration, experience, energies, and resources in the interest of peace. Participants saw reconciliation as resting fundamentally on a foundation of social justice and equity, and with a multitude of connections to the Millennium Development Goals (MDGs) and the broader development agenda.

CHANGING ROOTS AND NATURE OF CONFLICT

History is replete with armed conflicts that have squandered energy, hope, and wealth in futile attempts to establish the sanctity of tribe, race, class, nation, and religion. Yet, such conflicts often paradoxically confirm the common basic needs and aspirations of people across culture and time. People everywhere want the chance for themselves and their children to succeed in an equitable world.

The nature of conflict was seen, nonetheless, in the reflections at Dublin, to have changed in fundamental ways over recent decades. The Cold War and decolonization eras saw many of the world's poorest countries beset by violence and instability, and their aftermath left patterns and paths to intervention that kept many latent conflicts simmering. The post–Cold War world has seen a dramatic rise in the incidence and duration of civil wars—conflicts far less defined by ideology or superpower rivalry. With the United States and the European Union now the largest power brokers, rapid shifts in the global geopolitics have altered the landscape of conflicts. Reverend Samuel Kobia noted, "We have seen the emergence of self-financed conflicts in Africa that have nothing to do with the Cold War, which have nothing to do with colonialism. . . . And their toll is particularly heavy on children and on women." Modern intrastate conflicts often result from underdevelopment and from the flaring of ethnic and religious rivalries, exacerbated by variable access to power and resources.

With September 11, 2001, the face of conflict mutated once again. Prince Turki Al-Faisal Al-Saud recalled that "dialogue and understanding between cultures and communities has come under further pressure by the evil of terrorism, which is associated with Islam but that goes against every principle of Islam. All terrorism, including suicide bombers, is a cardinal sin in Islam." Countries attempting to wage war on terror confront an often-unfamiliar spectrum of nonstate actors, and their ability to monitor these groups—whose positions often reflect popular views—has proven polarizing both within and among countries.

There was a call for a stronger commitment to multilateral alliances in strengthening international security. Prince Turki observed that "after September 11, 2001, the concept of international security changed. Cold War confrontation and containment have been replaced by a tendency to respond to international crises through unilateral intervention."

Mary Robinson noted that "as UN High Commissioner for Human Rights, I pleaded against a broad war on terrorism, as this has actually worked against a collective approach to bringing the perpetrators of these horrible crimes against humanity to justice."

Bishop Gunnar Staalsett highlighted the looming threat of chemical and nuclear warfare from governments and terrorist networks alike in this new multipolar environment: "The number of nuclear powers has expanded, and, with the threat of terrorism, there is even some possibility of nuclear power going astray. The tsunami was a disaster caused by nature. A nuclear war will be caused by human beings. . . . In the aftermath of a nuclear tsunami, we would not be speaking about reclaiming land within 10 years, but rather of reclaiming lives over many generations."

Hopes for the global effort to fight poverty were seen as fundamentally challenged by this pattern of continuing conflict: insurgency in Iraq; too slow progress in Afghanistan; suicide bombings a constant risk in many parts of the world; and Indonesia, Saudi Arabia, Spain, and Turkey all reeling from recent attacks. Despite some optimism sparked by the transfer of power within the Palestine Liberation Organization, few observers predicted near-term resolution of the Israeli and Palestinian conflict. Bitter civil wars have torn apart Angola, Liberia, Mozambique, Sierra Leone, Sri Lanka, and Yugoslavia; ethnic divisions have devastated the Balkans, Burundi, and Rwanda. The global picture of the devastation inflicted by such conflicts is staggering. They have killed some 4 million people over the past decade and left more than 100 million people chronically malnourished.[2] Violence has impoverished countries in every major region, sometimes wiping out decades of economic and social development and, in other cases, preventing development from taking hold. Wars have destroyed infrastructure, disrupted trade links, and decimated institutional capacity. Conflict severely undermines the ability of countries to foster social justice and to sustain the basic conditions of stability, with the ultimate result that countries can become trapped in vicious cycles of violence and poverty. Only by examining the full panoply of human suffering that is the legacy of militarized and divided societies—from the dramatic increase in mortality, to the suffering of millions of refugees, to the violence perpetrated against women—can we appreciate the appalling scale of destruction.

The Dublin group called for a new moral and sociopolitical consensus behind the MDGs, comparable in its vision and depth to the post–World War II period and the founding of the United Nations. It is vitally important that the MDGs be understood as fundamentally linked to the quest for peace.

DEVELOPMENT DIMENSIONS OF CONFLICT

While every country struggles with internal political, ethnic, and religious tension, countries plagued by underdevelopment and poverty face a far higher risk that these tensions will degenerate into instability and violence. That 15 of the world's 20 poorest countries today have suffered from a major conflict in the past 15 years bears painful testament to this proposition.[3] Many of these countries find themselves increasingly left behind by the advancing global economy, with violence and instability standing as persistent obstacles to economic and social advancement.

While interstate conflicts usually attract media attention, intrastate conflict and civil wars are actually more common. From 1989 to 1997, 88 of 103 conflicts around the globe were purely domestic, with another 9 classified as "intrastate, with foreign intervention."[4] Since 1990, nearly every country in Africa has experienced a civil war or borders a nation that has.[5] Countries such as Rwanda, plagued by genocide and ethnic conflict, remain at the margins of the global community, victimized by weak institutions and inadequate social services and dependent on outside aid. Countries emerging from war have more than a 40 percent chance of relapse within five years; such countries can take a generation or more to return to prewar conditions.[6] Moreover, as Mary Robinson recalled (citing her personal experience with the conflicts in Ireland), civil conflicts often ignite easily and quickly, but once started can take a very long time to extinguish.

The changing landscape of conflict—the rising incidence and deep economic roots of civil tension, combined with the proliferation of small arms—has added significantly to the scope and duration of global conflict. The tragic results are that the threshold of engagement has been lowered, state institutions have been weakened, illegal activities have proliferated, and the scale of devastation wrought by civil conflict has dramatically grown. Alarming quantities of small arms continue to flow to disaffected groups throughout the world, including, disturbingly, young children forced into combat. Tragically, in some war-torn countries, more children know how to shoot than to read.

Although each civil conflict results from a unique nexus of economic, political, social, religious, and historical conditions, these factors are tightly associated with economic development. Economic underdevelopment, poverty, and social exclusion are both causes and consequences of conflict. When festering tensions flare into violence, they also erase years and even decades of development efforts and decimate economic and social institutions, with the result that poverty becomes ever more firmly entrenched.

The rising incidence of civil conflict over the past decade, along with the economic devastation and social tragedy that result, are now among the most critical development challenges facing the world's poorest nations. Indeed, the World Bank has devoted some 16 percent of its lending over the past few years to mitigating the effects of war, with significant roles in Afghanistan, Africa's Great Lakes region, the Balkans, Iraq, Liberia, Nepal, Sierra Leone, Timor Leste, the West Bank and Gaza, and other conflict-ridden areas.[7]

The world devotes staggering resources—some $1,000 billion dollars annually—to armaments and military activity, in marked contrast to annual development aid of some $65 billion. Prince Turki observed that "it is our collective disgrace that more effort and energy, and most important more resources, are allocated to conflict than to fighting poverty." Many asserted that resources spent on arms and conflicts would do more for peace if channeled to eradicating poverty.

EFFECTS OF CONFLICT HAVE MANY FACES

A central feature of modern civil war is a dramatic rise in civilian casualties; today only a small fraction of those affected by conflicts are soldiers. Whereas some 90 percent of victims during the twentieth century were military personnel, civilians (including women and children) have accounted for 90 percent of war casualties over the past decades.[8] Mary Robinson stressed the particularly ruinous toll that wars take on women; other participants recalled the horror stories of countless women who have survived rape even in refugee camps, of mass killings and of fundamentally brutalizing violence across conflict-shattered societies.

Although civil wars typically last five to seven years (some civil conflicts in Africa, such as in Angola and Sudan, have lasted decades), social and economic costs can linger for generations. Damage to the health care system, combined with malnutrition and illness, can cause high mortality rates long after violence ends. In some protracted conflicts, whole generations—both in urban and rural areas—may forgo their chance for education. A more intangible effect is the lasting fear that violence generates. Intimate exposure to brutality often leaves individuals psychologically scarred for their lifetimes and, in many instances, may scar the lifetimes of succeeding generations as those memories are passed on.

Because war leaves behind a divided and embittered population and destroys or weakens economic and social institutions, it heightens the risk of future violence. The economic devastation also impedes development and, thus, worsens the poverty that led to the initial war. Nations can, thus, be caught in a vicious and seemingly interminable cycle of persistent poverty and violence.

Damage caused by armed conflict ripples out in ever-broader rings, affecting the region and, ultimately, the global community. Massive floods of refugees from prolonged civil wars migrating into neighboring nations can affect entire regions. In 2001, the United Nations High Commission for Refugees assisted about 12 million refugees who had crossed national boundaries and some 5.3 million people who had become displaced within their own countries. Most were fleeing conflicts in the world's poorest countries. Refugees pick up diseases and spread them throughout refugee camps and the population surrounding those camps. The problem is compounded by the near complete absence of medical care in conflict-affected areas.

Mass rape and mass flight contribute heavily to the HIV/AIDS pandemic, as do the breakdown in the family and social structures that otherwise limit risky behavior. Displacement adds significantly to the number of persons living in abject poverty, while a tide of refugees can strain the resources of nations attempting to provide basic shelter and humanitarian assistance. Add to this a sharp decline in foreign investment in a broad swath of countries in regions with armed conflict, and the result is an overall slowing of regional development and a heightened risk that conflict may also escalate in neighboring nations. Ultimately, although difficult to quantify, the world feels the ripple effect of war in any country or region. Insecurity presents a drag on the global economy, as resources, which might have gone toward longer-term development, instead go toward emergency humanitarian assistance or other immediate relief interventions.

The production and sale of hard drugs and the escalation of conflict are mutually reinforcing. Recent research has suggested that 95 percent of the production of hard drugs occurs in countries undergoing civil war, since conflict gives traffickers the territory essential to producing vast quantities of drug crops.[9] In Afghanistan and Colombia, these crops have often been used to finance rebel groups.

Terrorism also relies on access to territory outside the control of government to flourish, while civil war produces a supply of weapons and disaffected youth from which terrorist organizations can draw. The poverty and conflict that fuel the growing threat from terrorist organizations are of clear global concern.

MEASURES TO PREVENT CONFLICT

Working together, the international development community, governments, and civil society—including faith leaders—can support social and economic policies that reduce poverty and make a society dramatically less prone to violence. Support for the difficult transition from war to peace must show quick and credible results to minimize the risk that conflict will reignite. Key components of the postconflict development agenda include demobilizing ex-combatants, including child soldiers; reintegrating refugees; removing land mines; and reestablishing government services, such as education and health care—all areas where faith-based organizations have a wealth of experience.

One important measure is curbing the official corruption that breeds disaffection and distrust: governments have a strong interest in showing that they are using revenue from natural resources, foreign aid, and taxes for the material benefit of all. Curbing corruption also gives governments more resources to implement economic policies and to deliver social services, thereby reducing the likelihood of violence. Here also, there is much scope for a greater role for faith and development leaders working in alliance.

Lorna Gold and Philip O'Brien underlined the importance of engaging youth both in preventing violence and in moving toward reconciliation. Philip O'Brien commented, "If we can start working with young people, we can deal with some of the causes of these conflicts. We have a responsibility to avoid talking just about our own generation, which is part of the problem. A colleague often describes war as the business of middle-aged men—and he emphasized men—the cost of which is borne by young people."

Swami Agivesh underscored the urgency of involving women: "Women's voices have been marginalized in resolving conflict. We need to tap the resources of women, which represent compassion. Because the victims of conflicts are mostly women and children, they understand and have a stake in the peacemaking."

A critical element of any postconflict agenda is reviving economic growth because it is so closely associated with a critical ingredient for peaceful and successful societies: hope. Countries need to create the basic conditions for reestablishing households and livelihoods by quickly channeling services to poor communities to convince displaced populations to return and resettle. With large numbers of people fearful of returning to their communities, the challenges of rebuilding those communities and of restarting agricultural growth may be staggering. This concern is especially true when unserviced international debt poses legal and political constraints that delay the resumption of international aid. There is much experience in overcoming such obstacles but the process remains complex and cumbersome—and it takes time. War also severely undermines prospects for foreign direct investment, and infrastructure suffers from neglect of routine maintenance, as well as from war-inflicted damage.

ROLES FOR FAITH LEADERS AND COMMUNITIES

Faced with this somber tapestry, the prophetic vocation of faith leaders is critical. (See box 5.1.) Faith institutions can play pivotal roles in easing tensions and creating an environment in which opposing factions cooperate and rebuild. At the community level, these leaders can provide physical relief and spiritual comfort, while at the policy-making level, they can help interpret conflicting information, shape public opinion, and facilitate the peace process.

The experience of the Community of Sant'Egidio in conflict situations is well known. Combining a long-term engagement with the poorest groups in the poorest societies, Sant'Egidio's approach has been to earn the trust of all sides to the conflict, which, in turn, has often allowed them to play a mediating and leadership role at crucial moments, thus bringing real knowledge of the situation on the ground.[10] Perhaps less well known

BOX 5.1. HANDLING CONFLICT WITH COMPASSION AND WISDOM

From the perspectives of Chinese philosophy and Indian Buddhism, harmony and conflict are two sides of the same issue, and both are normal. In Chinese philosophy, the interaction between yin and yang—and the interplay among the five elements of metal, wood, water, fire, and earth—entails both conflict and cooperation. Conflicts result when these elements are in opposition. Prosperity results when they cooperate. Buddhism advocates *dependent origination,* in which all phenomena in our lives and the universe arise and perish owing to causes and conditions. These phenomena, be they natural, social, physical, biological or psychological, are filled with contradiction as well as compromise.

How should we face these challenges? We should handle all matters with wisdom and should treat all people with compassion. Not creating troubles for oneself is wisdom; not causing harm to others is compassion. Adjusting one's attitude and looking at reality is wisdom. Treating others with tolerance and empathy is compassion. With wisdom, vexations do not arise; with compassion, one has no enemies.

Our perceptions of contradiction and conflict, evil and injustice, suffering and happiness, fortune and misfortune, and poverty and affluence may differ from person to person, place to place, and one time period to another. While efforts to seek justice from the national environment, social environment, different people and groups, family members, and relationships can yield some positive results, external conflicts—as well as contradictions within oneself—will continue. Once one adjusts one's attitude and viewpoint, one's anger and sense of injustice will dissolve. With inner peace comes happiness.

—The Most Venerable Master Sheng Yen

have been the efforts of Religions for Peace, which, with patience and persistence, also works to bring the joined voices—and hands—of faith leaders into efforts to bring about peace and reconciliation, witness their recent work in Liberia.[11]

Drawing on his vast experience with the Community of Sant'Egidio in mediating conflicts, Mario Giro offered guidelines for civil society and faith-based groups working to resolve conflict and to defuse mounting social tension:

> First, unlike government officials, who cannot sit in the bush for months, we have time to listen to all the tales of injustice. Second, we have to create a framework for nonthreatening mediation and accept that we cannot immediately judge these tales, because if we imagine we can impose a peace process, we are on the wrong path. Finally—again unlike government ministers—faith-based organizations can afford to be wrong. We have to accept the possibility of failure and remember that we are dealing with a pathology of memories and identities.

For groups hovering on the edge of despair and hopelessness, faith leaders can provide succor, relief, and solidarity. Yet, participants also recognized that religious differences often lie at the core of conflict and that the role of religion differs fundamentally from situation to situation. Swami Agnivesh noted that "religions sometimes start with a position of self-righteousness and built-in arrogance" that can foster conflict or inhibit reconciliation; self-criticism and true spirituality are needed to counter these tendencies. Master Sheng Yen suggested that religious conflicts are the most deep-seated and difficult to resolve.

Lord Carey agreed that "we have to acknowledge that faith issues contribute to conflict," but he also posed the critical next question: "What are the resources within religious traditions that will enable resolution of conflict?" With notions of justice deeply embedded in Christianity, Islam, Judaism, Buddhism, and Hinduism, religious leaders are uniquely placed to act against injustice and inequality, to prevent conflict, and to pave the way for reconciliation. Faith leaders can break down walls between ethnic and religious groups by moving away from the "us-versus-them" approach. Assuming the role of mediator can pose a significant challenge to faith leaders. (See box 5.2.)

BOX 5.2. ROLE OF PROPHETS

The approach of the Hebrew prophets depended upon the context in which they addressed the people. In a situation of insecurity and alienation, they saw their primary role as one of nurturing group identity, [thus] imparting a sense of security and hope. The prophets challenged people who were secure in their land to be righteous and respond to those who were marginalized and vulnerable. But when they were in exile, living in vulnerable situations, the prophets focused less on telling people to be more conscious of the needs of others or to reach out to the poor; rather, [they] saw their role as providing succor [by] strengthening identity and purpose. Similarly, today differing contexts and realities need to be taken into account.

—*Rabbi David Rosen*

Reverend William Vendley noted that "students of conflict recognize that identity, whether religious, ethnic, tribal, clan, or geographic, is the perceived basis for injustice. Political and religious leadership can either exacerbate those differences or try to address them. The unique dimension of religion is a stunning ability to pierce the "scapegoating" dynamic that is exacerbated by group identity, injustice, and cunning and sometimes by unscrupulous political leaders."

There are countless inspiring examples of what is possible when faith groups come together and when they join their wisdom and experience with those of other partners. Citing the agonizing conflict in Sierra Leone, Reverend Vendley recounted how a Muslim-Christian council withstood the efforts of rebel groups to divide it, then played a key role in mediating peace, and ultimately facilitated community-level reconciliation. Reverend William Lesher drew attention to the longstanding, cruel conflict in northern Uganda, a conflict largely ignored by the world community. There, the interfaith Acholi Religious Leaders Peace Initiative has promoted dialogue between the government and the Lord's Resistance Army. Because sons and daughters are engaged on both sides, the leaders have conveyed to all that "we are killing ourselves as long as we participate in these struggles." Their mediation work has continued for more than eight years with a misleadingly simple objective: to build trust and bring people to the table.

As the Dublin group explored concrete, constructive paths ahead, many stressed the importance of objectivity, self-criticism and analysis, and, most important, generosity of spirit and in-depth knowledge of specific circumstances. Rabbi David Rosen highlighted the value of "striving for clarity in terms of definition and in understanding context, because religions vary enormously in terms of their character and their role in different places and situations." Reverend Kobia spoke to what he termed transformative justice: "Justice transforms both the victim and the perpetrator. Unless we deal with that, we will be unable to deal with conflicts in a holistic manner."

Mary Robinson highlighted the potentially powerful role of truth and reconciliation commissions, underscoring that they are characterized by unique combinations of high levels of sophistication, remarkable humility, and respect for all factions of a conflict. Yet they are almost always underfunded, despite useful roles they have played in many situations.

Communication and understanding came at the center of the discussion. Hany El Banna cited the speed of modern communications, whereby "people on the streets of Delhi or Jakarta know in three minutes what is happening in New York." It puts an added onus on government and other leaders (including faith leaders) to be respectful in their approach to other people and cultures. Mr. El Banna added, "Do not undermine or underestimate the capabilities and the intellectual capacities of the masses in different parts of the world. Let dialogue have authority on the people, on the economists, on the politicians, so that it can also affect the mentality of decision makers themselves."

Prince Turki noted, "Dialogue is the only way to bring about a culture of peace and tolerance, to develop respect for one another. We need to celebrate the diversity of our world cultures as a source of richness rather than of division and conflict. Positive dialogue and good friendships are based on trust."

Archbishop Gregorios Ibrahim agreed:

Dialogue, serious dialogue, is the most important challenge we face in this phase of our history. Dialogue between civilizations and dialogue between religions. But the dialogue must be characterized by a human and a spiritual dimension. How can we find the common denominators in the teachings of the religious books from Islam, from Christianity and from Judaism? Only then can we concentrate on what brings us together and begin to constitute a basis for a world of peaceful cohabitation and brotherhood.

Dialogue—the ability to listen and to empathize—is a daunting and long-term challenge. Among the most moving interventions were those that articulated, passionately and provocatively, how profoundly difficult real reconciliation can be, especially where tensions have existed over long periods. Rabbi Rosen observed that

> [i]n situations of conflict, nobody sees themselves as the oppressors. Everybody sees themselves as victims. The language we use is important, because if we try to demonize people on one side or the other, it will compound the conflict. . . . In the Middle East, where I live, everyone sees themselves as vulnerable and victimized. Palestinians see themselves as the victims of Israeli might and power. And Israel sees itself as the victim in the face of Arab hostility. Everyone is caught up in the victim syndrome. If we have this mentality, we cannot make a constructive contribution. It is artificial and illusory to assume that shared values in themselves will be able to bring an end to conflict.

Master Sheng Yen recounted a visit to Israel and Palestine two years earlier: "I discovered that both sides felt very strongly that they had been wronged and treated very unfairly. But I also discovered that while both sides often used the same terminology, even the word *peace* had quite different interpretations."

Faith organizations have repeatedly shown a stalwart commitment in the face of conflict, regardless of personal danger. Faith-based organizations are often the sole source of education and heath services in war-ravaged and isolated communities, and their involvement has sometimes even shifted the course of negotiations. Rabbi Rosen observed, "Secular political leadership has tried to exclude religious groups from conflict resolution. When one sees how mercilessly religion has been abused, you can understand that. But it is a tragic mistake, because if you don't want religion to be part of the problem, it has to be part of the solution."

NOTES

1. Olivier McTernan, *Violence in God's Name: Religion in an Age of Conflict* (Maryknoll, NY: Orbis Books, 2003). This is one of a lengthy list of titles exploring the same topic; Jessica Stern's *Terror in the Name of God: Why Religious Militants Kill* (New York: HarperCollins Books, 2003) is another prominent example.

2. Clare Short, "Security, Development, and Conflict Prevention," speech given to the Royal College of Defence Studies, May 13, 1998, citing the Carnegie Commission.

3. *Post-Conflict Reconstruction: The Role of the World Bank* (Washington, DC: World Bank, 1998).

4. Ibid.

5. Ibid.

6. Ibid.

7. See the World Bank Web site "Conflict Prevention and Reconstruction" at http://lnweb18.worldbank.org/ESSD/sdvext.nsf/67ByDocName/Conflict PreventionandReconstruction.

8. Paul Collier, V. L. Elliot, Havard Hegre, Anke Hoeffler, Marta Reynal-Querol, and Nicholas Sambanis, *Breaking the Conflict Trap: Civil War and Development Policy,* Policy Research Report (Washington, DC: World Bank and Oxford University Press, 2003).

9. Ibid.

10. See Sant'Egidio Web site for further information (http://www.santegidio.org/ en/index.html) and descriptions of the organization's work in Katherine Marshall and Lucy Keough, *Mind, Heart, and Soul in the Fight Against Poverty* (Washington, DC: World Bank, 2004).

11. World Conference of Religions for Peace Web site: http://www.wcrp.org/.

Bishop Gunnar Staalsett and James D. Wolfensohn

Akbar Ahmed and Rev. William Vendley

The Path

Like my Sunni ancestors

Inspired by the blood and traditions of the Prophet

I am on a journey

With others walking along side

Some taking the help of imams and ayatollahs

Others the law of Moses or the love of Jesus

Yonder

I see those who find the divine in the Ganga

Or on top of the Himalayas

They find the divine in the noble doings of Lord Ram

Yet others find other paths

I wish them all Godspeed

For all of them are part of the "tribes and nations"

That the Quran tells me I must love

So that I can love the divine

—Akbar Ahmed
February 2005

Press conference: *(l to r)* Hany El Banna, Lord George Carey, Mary Robinson, Archbishop Diarmuid Martin, Thoraya Obaid, James D. Wolfensohn

CHAPTER

The Way Forward

As we look to the future, this assemblage will stand as a most important junction, a place of dialogue, a place of encounter, for honest exchange and challenge, but also where we sought and found consensus on basic principles.

—Bishop Gunnar Staalsett

Seven years after Jim Wolfensohn and Lord George Carey launched a dialogue involving faith and development leaders, participants concluded that faith-development partnerships stood at a crossroads. This stance sparked much reflection and discussion during the Dublin meeting about where the road might lead after Dublin.

Jim Wolfensohn framed the stakes for the group:

I believe there are two possibilities. One is to agree that this has been a great experience, that we have improved understanding between faith-based organizations and international and national financial institutions, and that we have established a basis for more dialogue and cooperation. We have also spurred interfaith dialogue on development, and fostered appreciation in development circles of the roles played by faith institutions. We could, therefore, declare victory and steal off into the night. A second possibility, though, is that we can aim for a more pragmatic and active path and set a new and concrete course of joint action.

The second option—the path toward a stronger, tangible alliance grounded in a sound institutional base—dominated discussion over the final day. No one was willing to countenance the option of drawing the process to a close, so all focused on how best to support and expand faith-development partnerships. As evidence of the need for such partnerships, Brizio Biondi-Morra pointed to Latin America, where income distribution is heavily skewed in favor of the rich, poverty is widespread, and crime is rampant in many countries. "To reach a scale that offers real progress, we need to collaborate in unconventional ways."

What could this alliance contribute, practically, to the global fight against poverty? Father Dominique Peccoud suggested that the real value of the alliance was in shifting development from a sole focus on materialism to a more values-based approach. Discussions of equity and other ethical challenges offer new avenues for enhancing policy decisions in many fields. Participants also saw a host of practical possibilities for expanding alliances on HIV/AIDS, engaging in national antipoverty strategies, and strengthening health policies and programs. Global circumstances make such faith-development collaboration especially vital: meeting the Millennium Development Goals (MDGs) will require all constituencies to engage in both policy making and specific programs.

Efforts to enhance global security also demand new forms of collaboration—most acutely in fostering understanding between Christian and Muslim communities. As Akbar Ahmed suggested, "So many Americans have no idea of the basic tenants of Islam but, nevertheless, are hostile to it. Anti-American sentiment in Muslim countries is even higher. When millions of people succumb to prejudice, hatred, and anger, and when so much of the Muslim world has abominable literacy rates and health indicators, a dialogue between faith and development leaders is not a luxury; it is a necessity."

Marcel Massé suggested that "after trying to stay apart for so long, faith and development organizations are slowly realizing that the world needs both sides—people who will implement projects, policies, and programs within pluralistic societies and people who will help to shape values. Unless people's minds and values change—and this is the role of faith-based organizations—we will not succeed." Archbishop Diarmuid Martin noted that the European Constitution requires the European Commission to establish a transparent dialogue with faith groups on a range of development issues. Some European countries, including Austria, Ireland, France, the Netherlands, Sweden, and the United Kingdom, are already doing so.

A surprising benefit of the faith-development dialogue has been greater communication among faith communities themselves. Metropolitan John of Pergamon observed that "much ecumenism has thus far focused on doctrinal differences. But religions need to consider the practical, moral, and ethical questions where they agree and where they differ, because the future of religious cooperation lies in ethics rather than dogma." Douglas Balfour suggested there is great value in "looking for faith-based organizations with the most traction in changing development policies, outcomes, and impact."

The Dublin group saw a revitalized World Faiths Development Dialogue (WFDD) as critical to sustaining the faith-development partnership. Despite its limited resources, that organization has grown from an informal coordinating office launched in 1998 to a more formal institution based in the United Kingdom. The group has built a remarkable global network of faith leaders engaged in advocacy and action on poverty and development, and has laid a foundation for dialogue between those faith communities and international development institutions.

As Cardinal Theodore McCarrick observed, "No other group is bringing faith-based institutions into direct dialogue with the World Bank and other international financial agencies. These face-to-face conversations are critical."

Akbar Ahmed concurred that "the WFDD is the only forum that brings a holistic approach to world issues." Participants endorsed the plan to shift WFDD's base to Washington, D.C., with a two-year window to attract a competent staff and to test its ability to meet its objectives of providing a forum for dialogue on critical policy issues for the fight against poverty, creating practical information tools, and advancing action in critical areas. Jean-Louis Sarbib noted that, although the World Bank has sought more holistic approaches to development, "perhaps they are not holistic enough, because they are often devoid of a spiritual dimension." (See box 6.1.)

While there was universal accord to continue the faith-development forum, there was also consideration of the need to adopt a more limited and focused agenda, without sacrificing the essence of the initiative, namely that it has been and should continue to be a forum for dialogue. Archbishop Martin summarized the challenge: "We have avoided calling

BOX 6.1. SOME CLOSING THOUGHTS

Archbishop Martin's definition of development—as a realization of everyone's God-given potential—resonates, and it is what many of us at the World Bank believe. We have sought more holistic definitions of development over recent years, but I realize, after these days together, that they may not be holistic enough, because they are often devoid of the spiritual dimension. You cannot speak of a holistic definition of development while leaving out the spiritual dimension.

For the future, the priority is for us to continue to learn to work more closely together: to make sure that neither the faiths intervene alone, although they can, nor the Bank intervenes alone, although it can. Rather, together we must try to find concrete answers, not only to questions about how to enable the poor to become the subjects of their own development, but also to questions we have about each other. We still have a wide series of differences—on debt cancellation, for example—and, because of these meetings over the past few years, we can talk about those differences and listen to each other.

The most important result of our dialogue, however, is that we work together to define and live a new orthodoxy for development that considers people as whole human beings with spiritual, as well as material, needs. If we can do this, we will have developed a truly new paradigm, one that entails listening to the voices of women and young people, because they are the ones who have not been heard enough. Wherever I have seen development really work, in the poorest parts of Africa, it is when women and young people have been an integral part of the process.

—Jean-Louis Sarbib

our efforts 'a World Faiths Development Organization' or a 'World Faiths Plan' for good reason; this process is about dialogue. But we need clearer, more concrete programs."

Rosemary Spencer added, "Dialogue is hugely valuable in itself, but the most important goal is to improve efforts on the ground for the poorest and most disadvantaged communities."

Given the expectation that WFDD will concentrate on specific development challenges of concern to development and faith institutions alike, the discussion turned to the question of priorities. Informal polling of the participants highlighted several core issues:

- *Children and Youth:* All agreed that WFDD should focus in this area. Specific concerns include street children, orphans, and other vulnerable children; employment and exploitation; and the MDG of universal primary education by 2015. Participants also cited the need to bring youth more fully into national and global debates on such concerns.
- *Gender:* The nexus among women, poverty, education, and overall development—as reflected in the MDGs—offers a kaleidoscope of possible directions for WFDD. Faith and development leaders and institutions share a vision of the need to empower women politically and socially, and of the resulting effect on alleviating poverty.
- *HIV/AIDS:* This group of faith and development leaders has always focused sharply on the pandemic. Faith-based organizations have a wealth of experience across a range of interventions. The Dublin meeting debated the relentless spread and persistent stigma of the disease and its impact on women and orphans, and agreed that these challenges should figure prominently in the work of the WFDD.
- *Environment:* The WFDD has not highlighted environmental issues per se, and participants urged it to engage them more directly. They specifically cited links between poverty reduction, climate change, water issues, and sustainable development.
- *Conflict:* Faith-based organizations have deep roots in efforts to prevent armed conflict, mediate peace, and enable societies to transition from war to peace. The Community of Sant'Egidio and Religions for Peace are two outstanding examples of such groups that have also par-

ticipated in this forum. Faith groups and development organizations could jointly address the critical concern of child soldiers. They could also collaborate on reconciliation and rebuilding, given that faith groups have fewer constraints on participating in the former, while development institutions have more technical and financial experience in promoting the latter.

Other pressing arenas for action include corruption, ethnic conflict, human trafficking, corporate social responsibility, and concrete measures of progress on the MDGs. Jim Wolfensohn counseled that "we should not try to address all global concerns, but rather agree on two or three 'tsunamis' a year that a small staff could highlight more effectively than faith-based and international financial institutions acting separately."

Participants called for responding quickly to "emerging tsunamis," and for maintaining connections to grassroots organizations and local communities to ensure that high-level debate among international leaders is practical and relevant. Lorna Gold stressed the importance of maintaining a dialogue in areas where faith and development organizations do not always agree, but where faith groups can contribute, including debt relief and the global financial architecture. Rajwant Singh cautioned that "many faith communities still lack the capacity to participate in a dialogue with the World Bank and other financial institutions because they do not speak their language."

Swami Agnivesh underscored that, in critiquing dominant development policies, the group must protect its core values, "including truth, love, compassion, and justice." He urged that "we maintain four nonnegotiable considerations based on equity and justice: no inequality between men and women; no inequality between black and white; no inequality between castes, high or low; and finally, no inequality based on birth."

(l to r) Lord George Carey, Mary Robinson, and Rajwant Singh

(l to r) Rajwant Singh; Gregorios Yohanna Ibrahim, Archbishop of Aleppo; Swami Agnivesh; Sahib Jathedar Manjit Singh

Participants in the Dublin Meeting

His Holiness Shri Swami Agnivesh is well known for his work in various fields of social work, social justice, and women's rights. He has chaired the United Nations Trust Fund on Contemporary Forms of Slavery and the Bandhua Mukti Morcha (Bonded Labour Liberation Front). Since November 2001, he has been president of the World Council of Arya Samaj, a spiritual and social organization. From 1977 to 1982, he served as a member of the Haryana Legislative Assembly and was minister of education of Haryana in 1979. Swami Agnivesh has published several books, including *Vedic Socialism* and *Religion, Spirituality, and Social Action*, as well as numerous articles on national social and political issues in leading newspapers and magazines. He received the Anti-Slavery International Award in 1990, the Freedom and Human Rights Award in 1994, and the Right Livelihood Award in 2004.

Professor Akbar Ahmed holds the Ibn Khaldun chair of Islamic studies at American University in Washington, D.C. He is on the board of directors of the American Council for the Study of Islamic Societies, as well as the editorial boards of several distinguished academic journals. He has been actively involved in interfaith dialogue and the study of global Islam and its effect on contemporary society. He is the author of several books on contemporary Islam, including *Discovering Islam: Making Sense of Muslim History and Society*, on which the British Broadcasting Corporation based its six-part television series *Living Islam*. He has held visiting professorships at Princeton, Harvard, and Cambridge universities. Professor Ahmed joined the civil service of Pakistan in 1966 and has held various posts in

Bangladesh and Pakistan. He served as Pakistani high commissioner to the United Kingdom from 1999 to 2000. He was appointed trustee of the World Faiths Development Dialogue by the Archbishop of Canterbury and, in 2003, was appointed a charter member of a national interfaith initiative that is based at the National Cathedral by the Bishop of Washington, D.C.

His Royal Highness Prince Turki Al-Faisal Al-Saud is Saudi Arabia's ambassador to the United Kingdom and Ireland. He chairs the King Faisal Center for Research and Islamic Studies and is a member of the board of trustees of the King Faisal Foundation. The Center for Research was founded in 1983 and, in keeping with the goals of the King Faisal Foundation, it is dedicated to serving Islamic civilization, supporting research, and encouraging cultural and scientific activities in a number of fields. In January 2004, Prince Turki and Lord George Carey became co-chairs of the Council of 100 Leaders (World Economic Forum), thereby promoting understanding and dialogue between the Western and Islamic worlds. Prince Turki has studied at Princeton, Cambridge, and Georgetown universities.

Tom Arnold has been chief executive of Concern Worldwide, Ireland's largest nongovernmental organization working in relief and development, since October 2001. Before joining Concern, Mr. Arnold worked in the Irish Department of Agriculture and Food for 13 years as chief economist and assistant secretary general. He has extensive international experience in agricultural and food policy in both the governmental and nongovernmental sectors. In April 2003, Mr. Arnold was appointed to the UN Hunger Task Force, one of several task forces set up by Secretary General Kofi Annan and Mark Malloch Brown, administrator of the UN Development Programme, which is charged with devising strategies for meeting the Millennium Development Goals by 2015.

Douglas Balfour is executive director of Integral, a new alliance of 12 Christian relief and development funding agencies around the world that are aiming to respond to disasters and long-term poverty. He is a driving force behind the Micah Challenge, which is a worldwide evangelical Christian campaign to halve global poverty by 2015 and is facilitated by the Micah Network (270 Christian development agencies from 70 countries) and the

World Evangelical Alliance. Beginning in October 1995, Mr. Balfour was general director of Tearfund UK, a Christian relief and development agency, which is part of the Integral network. In his nine years with Tearfund, he traveled to more than 40 developing countries, including Afghanistan, Argentina, Cambodia, Haiti, and Liberia. From 1989 to 1991, Mr. Balfour was an organizational consultant with Youth with a Mission, an international Christian youth movement. In 1991–92, he directed Medair's relief aid program in Liberia, running a psychological rehabilitation program for war-traumatized children and a program to provide essential drugs. Medair is a nongovernmental organization that was founded in 1988 and is inspired by Christian values to respond to suffering victims of war and disaster.

His All Holiness Ecumenical Patriarch Bartholomew is the spiritual leader of 300 million Orthodox Christians worldwide. Since ascending to the ecumenical throne in November 1991, he has pursued messages of spiritual revival; Orthodox unity; Christian reconciliation; interfaith tolerance and coexistence; protection of the environment; and a world united in peace, justice, and solidarity. As Ecumenical Patriarch of Constantinople, he has helped the church expand on many fronts. He has advanced Orthodox relations with Roman Catholics, Lutherans, Baptists, and other denominations, and he has taken an active role in strengthening relations with national Orthodox churches throughout Eastern Europe, including Russia, through direct visits. Known in Europe as "the Green Patriarch," Ecumenical Patriarch Bartholomew has been especially active in his concern for the environment.

Brizio Biondi-Morra is chair and CEO of the AVINA Foundation, which supports education, leadership development, and the environment in Latin America. AVINA has launched a major initiative to support Jesuit work in education. He also chairs the Board of Fundes International, which is part of the Schmidheiny Group and aims to improve the lot of small entrepreneurs in Latin America through access to credit, training, and consulting services. Mr. Biondi-Morra initially worked in archaeology and on films in Africa, and then he pursued business after studying at the Harvard Business School. He directed the Central American Business School before joining the Schmidheiny Group.

Chanel Boucher has been vice president for planning, policy, and research at the African Development Bank since January 2002. He joined the bank in 1996 as vice president for corporate services after working in key positions for the Canadian government. Beginning in 1971, he served as director general and then assistant deputy minister for finance and administration of the Ministry of Energy, Mines, and Resources; then he was assistant deputy minister of corporate services of the Ministry of Natural Resources.

Lord George Carey was enthroned as the 103rd Archbishop of Canterbury in April 1991, and he retired from that position in November 2002. The Archbishop is *primus inter pares* among the primates of the 70 million–strong worldwide Anglican community and, as such, was expected to maintain the unity of the communion. He played a key role in relationships with other denominations and faiths in the United Kingdom and throughout the world, visiting more than 90 countries. Lord Carey chairs the board of trustees of the World Faiths Development Dialogue and is a member of the Foundation Board of the World Economic Forum. In January 2004, he became co-chair of the Council of 100 Leaders (World Economic Forum) with Prince Turki Al-Faisal Al-Saud, promoting understanding and dialogue between the Western and Islamic worlds. He now works with the Christian relief and development agency Tearfund. Lord Carey was ordained as a priest in 1963 and served parishes in London and Durham, United Kingdom. He was a lecturer in theology in London and Nottingham, and also served as the principal of Trinity College in Bristol before becoming Bishop of Bath and Wells in 1987. After his retirement as Archbishop, Lord Carey was named first chancellor of the University of Gloucestershire. He is the author of many books on theological issues, including *The Gate of Glory*, as well as *Why I Believe in a Personal God: The Credibility of Faith in a Doubting Culture* and a recent autobiography, *Know the Truth*.

Monsignor Frank J. Dewane is undersecretary for the Pontifical Council for Justice and Peace, an organ of the Holy See, and often represents the Vatican at international events. The council aims to promote justice and peace worldwide in the light of the Gospel and the social teachings of the

Catholic Church. Its primary work is to engage in action-oriented studies that are based on both the papal magisterium and social teachings of the Church. The council collaborates with all those within the Church who are seeking the same ends and issues documents on topics such as international debt, environmental habitats, racism, international arms trade and land distribution, genetically modified organisms, and water.

Hany El Banna is president of Islamic Relief (UK) Worldwide, established in 1984 as an independent international relief and development organization. Mr. El Banna has consistently aimed to create greater understanding among Christians, Jews, and Muslims. He is a member of the Three Faiths Forum, which encourages friendship, goodwill, and understanding among these three Abrahamic monotheistic faiths, and he speaks and broadcasts on faith and development issues in Britain and abroad. He has spoken before the UK House of Commons on humanitarian aid, and the Foreign and Commonwealth Office on open dialogue as part of a tolerant foreign policy. Mr. El Banna is actively involved in the peace process in South Sudan, and he was awarded an Officer of the British Empire in the diplomatic service and overseas section from Queen Elizabeth II in 2004.

Nambar Enkhbayar was the prime minister of Mongolia until August 2004 and is now speaker of the Mongolian Parliament. He is a prominent Buddhist leader. Prime Minister Enkhbayar pioneered environmental and development policies in Mongolia that drew upon Buddhist teachings and practice. In June 2003, he was appointed international president of the Alliance of Religions and Conservation (ARC) trustees for three years. ARC is a secular body that helps the major world religions develop environmental programs based on their core teachings, beliefs, and practices. Mr. Enkhbayar has studied at the Moscow University of Literature and at Leeds University, United Kingdom. He was translator-editor and then head of the department at the Union of Mongolian Writers, vice president of the Mongolian Association of Translators, deputy chair of the Committee on Culture and Art, and Mongolia's minister for culture and art. His political career began in 1992. He was elected to the National Parliament in 1997 and was reelected in the national election of 2000, after which he became the 21st prime minister of Mongolia.

Ekaterina Genieva is executive director of the Open Society Institute (OSI) in Moscow. Part of the Soros Foundation, OSI aims to promote open societies by shaping government policy and supporting education, media, public health, and human and women's rights, as well as social, legal, and economic reform. She is also on the board of directors of the Soros Foundation. Since the fall of the Soviet Union, Ms. Genieva has been director of the All-Russia State Library for Foreign Literature and a leader of cultural reform. She is a member of various foundations and societies, including being vice president of the Russian Federation of Library Associations and a board member of the Russian Bible Society and the All-Russian Culture Foundation. Ms. Genieva is also affiliated with numerous international organizations. She is the author of many publications in the fields of English and Irish literature and has received numerous international awards. She holds honorary degrees from several universities, including the University of Illinois at Urbana-Champaign.

Mario Giro is head of the International Department of the Community of Sant'Egidio, where he was previously head of the West African section. The community is a Christian lay association that began in Rome in 1968 and is committed to serving the poor and dispossessed. It now operates in more than 70 countries with some 40,000 member-volunteers struggling against poverty and fostering peace and dialogue. The community pursues a wide range of activities, from local services (serving children, elderly, handicapped, refugees, immigrants and gypsies, AIDS, prisoners, and the homeless), to intervention on humanitarian grounds, to development projects and peace programs. Following the tragic events of September 11, 2001, the community launched an interfaith dialogue aimed at strengthening solidarity between Christianity and Islam, as well as at showing sympathy for the victims of terrorism. Its international meetings call for annual renewal of dialogue and understanding among the great world religions.

Lorna Gold is a senior policy analyst with Trócaire, the official overseas development agency of the Catholic Church in Ireland. Trócaire aims to support long-term development projects, provide relief during emergencies, and inform the Irish public about the root causes of poverty. Before joining Trócaire, she was with the Department of Politics at the University of York, United Kingdom. She is a specialist in international politics and follows United Nations processes closely.

Lord Brian Griffiths was appointed vice chair of Goldman Sachs International and international adviser to Goldman Sachs in 1991. He is concerned with strategic issues in the United Kingdom, European, and Asian operations, as well as with business development activities worldwide. He is also chair of Land Securities Trillium and is a non-executive director of Times Newspaper Holdings Ltd.; Herman Miller Inc.; ServiceMaster; and English, Welsh, and Scottish Railway. From 1991 to 1993, Lord Griffiths chaired the School Examination and Assessment Council, and from 1991 to 2000, he chaired the Centre for Policy Studies. He is also chair of the Archbishop of Canterbury's Lambeth Trust and Christian Responsibility in Public Affairs, and he has written extensively and lectures on ethics and business. Lord Griffiths taught at the London School of Economics from 1965 to 1976 and was appointed professor of banking and international finance at City University in 1976. He was dean of City University Business School from 1982 to 1985, was a director of the Bank of England, and then served as head of the prime minister's policy unit from 1985 to 1990.

Simon Xavier Guerrand-Hermès chairs the Guerrand-Hermès Foundation for Peace, founded in 1996 to increase global understanding and compassion by promoting education, livelihood, peace, youth, and interfaith dialogue. Mr. Guerrand-Hermès is also a director and vice chair of the Paris-based family boutique House of Hermès in the United States. He is internationally known for his study of religion, and he serves on the dean's council of Harvard Divinity School with other Harvard graduates and leaders who support the study of comparative religions. Mr. Guerrand-Hermès is the treasurer of the World Conference of Religions for Peace and chairs its Finance Committee.

Graham Hacche has been deputy director of the International Monetary Fund's External Relations Department since 1999. He joined the IMF in 1982 and has held a variety of positions as an economist. In the early

1990s, he was the speechwriter for IMF Managing Director Michel Camdessus, and from 1995 to 1999, he was the chief of the World Economic Studies Division in the Research Department, leading the team responsible for producing the IMF's twice-yearly World Economic Outlook. Before joining the IMF, Mr. Hacche worked for 10 years as an economist at the Bank of England while also consulting for the Organisation for Economic Co-operation and Development (OECD).

Haruhisa Handa is a private businessman and philanthropist who is active in the arts and in introducing Japanese cultural arts to the world. He chairs the International Foundation for Arts and Culture and has sponsored various artistic activities, including calligraphy exhibitions and operas, concerts, and Noh performances throughout the world. Recognized for his contributions to the Cambodian nation, he received an award from the Kingdom of Cambodia in January 2003. He built a hospital in Cambodia and runs it in collaboration with a local Christian group. He established Cambodia's first Japanese Culture and Business Research Center at the Cambodia Institute for Cooperation and Peace, the country's only national research facility, and he was chancellor of Cambodia University, the country's first private university. Mr. Handa is also president of the World Blind Golf Association, honorary chair of the Japan Blind Golf Association, vice chair of the Sihanouk Hospital Association, and vice chair of the International Shinto Foundation (a UN-accredited nongovernmental organization), among many other organizations. He operates several international companies.

Jeremy Harris was appointed the Archbishop of Canterbury's secretary for public affairs in 1998. As secretary, he is the senior lay adviser to the Church of England and the Archbishop. He deals with the Archbishop's calendar and relations with Downing Street and Parliament, businesses, and the media. Mr. Harris joined the British Broadcasting Corporation in 1974. In 1982, he became Madrid correspondent and was later posted to Moscow and Washington.

Gregorios Yohanna Ibrahim, Archbishop of Aleppo in the Syrian Orthodox Church, studied in Rome and promotes dialogue both among Christians and between Muslims and Christians. He is a member in the World Council of Churches and has worked to spread interfaith dialogue between Christians and Muslims, which he believes is critical in today's world.

Reverend Canon Ted Karpf is currently serving with the World Health Organization. He previously served as provincial canon missioner, Office of HIV/AIDS Community Ministries and Mission, of the Anglican Church of the Province of South Africa. Through his work with Archbishop Njongonkulu Ndungane, Archbishop of Cape Town, and as a leading spokesperson on HIV/AIDS, he has raised awareness of the pandemic among the wider Anglican Communion and has developed strategies and programs to address it. Reverend Karpf was a founder of the National Episcopal AIDS Coalition in 1988 and served as executive director from June 1993 through January 1998, advocating AIDS awareness through the slogan "the Episcopal Church has AIDS." He had abundant experience with AIDS in Dallas, Texas, where as Rector of St. Thomas the Apostle he buried 150 AIDS victims.

Reverend Dr. Samuel M. Kobia was appointed general secretary of the World Council of Churches (WCC) in January 2004, the first African to hold the position. The WCC brings together more than 340 churches, denominations, and fellowships in more than 100 countries and territories representing some 500 million Christians. Reverend Kobia is an ordained minister in the Methodist Church in Kenya. In 2003, he served as the WCC's special representative for Africa. In 2000, he spent a sabbatical as a fellow at the Center for the Study of Values in Public Life at Harvard Divinity School, exploring the religious and social values that inform churches' involvement in the democratization process in Africa. In September 1987, Reverend Kobia was appointed general secretary of the National Council of Churches Kenya (NCCK), and he helped promulgate the 1992 amendment of the Kenya Constitution that reintroduced a multiparty political system. He served for three years as NCCK's director of church development activities. He has published several articles and books focusing on economic development, debt relief, and violence prevention.

Satish Kumar is president of Schumacher College, United Kingdom, an international center for ecological studies. He is also the editor of *Resurgence*, an international magazine promoting peace, nonviolence, ecology, sustainability, organic agriculture, appropriate technology, and holistic philosophy. Mr. Kumar has campaigned for land reform in India and has actively participated in a number of peace movements, including walking from India to America from 1962 to 1964. In 1968, he established the London School of Non-Violence to teach Gandhian passive resistance to the youth of Europe. In November 2001, he received the Jamnalal Bajaj International Award for "promoting Gandhian values abroad." Mr. Kumar published his autobiography *Path without Destination* in 1999, and *You Are, Therefore, I Am* in September 2002.

Conor Lenihan is Irish minister of state for development cooperation and human rights, a position he has held since October 2004. He was first elected to the Irish Parliament in 1997. Prior to Mr. Lenihan's appointment, he was a radio broadcaster. He also served as political correspondent at Westminster for the *Irish News* and was a full-time public representative and former senior executive with Esat Digifone, a prominent communications company in Ireland.

Reverend Dr. William Lesher chairs the executive committee of the Council for a Parliament of the World's Religions. The council aims to cultivate harmony among the world's religious and spiritual communities and to foster engagement with other institutions to achieve a peaceful, just, and sustainable world. He has had a long career promoting global interfaith dialogue. Reverend Lesher joined the International Board of Consultants of the Parliament's Forum in 2003. From 1978 to 1997, he was president of the Lutheran School of Theology in Chicago, where he established the Chicago Center for Religion and Science. Before that, he served with the World Council of Churches in Geneva and was president of Pacific Lutheran Theological Seminary in Berkeley, California. He is the initiator of and an adviser to the Common Ground for the Common Good, sponsored by the National Council of Churches, the U.S. Catholic Conference, and the Synagogue Council of America, and he chairs the Task Force on Globalization of Theological Education for the Association of Theological

Schools. He is also a member of the United Board for Christian Higher Education in Asia and a member of the editorial board of *Zygon,* a journal of religion and science.

Christopher Long is the acting director of the World Faiths Development Dialogue (WFDD). WFDD aims to facilitate dialogue and common action on poverty and development among people from different religions, and between them and international development institutions. He is a retired British diplomat who served as ambassador to Switzerland (1988–92), Egypt (1992–95), and Hungary (1995–98).

Reverend Canon Richard Marsh directs the Education Centre at Canterbury Cathedral, with a particular focus on the cathedral's International Study Centre. As canon librarian, he is responsible for the cathedral's archives, as well as its ancient library, which is becoming a working theological resource in association with Canterbury Christ Church University College and the St. Augustine's Foundation. From 1995 to 2001, Canon Marsh was director for ecumenical affairs in the office of the Archbishop of Canterbury at Lambeth Palace. He also chaired the board of trustees of the World Faiths Development Dialogue.

Katherine Marshall is director and counselor to the president of the World Bank. She heads the Development Dialogue on Values and Ethics Division, the unit responsible for engaging with faith-based institutions around development issues and for forging partnerships with organizations addressing the complex ethical issues of globalization. Ms. Marshall has worked on development issues for more than 30 years, focusing on fighting poverty and bringing gender and civil society issues into the spotlight. She has been a country director in the Africa Region of the World Bank and has served as director of social policy and governance for the Bank's East Asia and Pacific Region during the 1997 Asian crisis. Ms. Marshall served as a founding trustee of the World Faiths Development Dialogue and as its interim chief executive. She has made numerous addresses at various international events and published several papers. Her latest book, *Mind, Heart, and Soul in the Fight against Poverty,* coedited with Lucy Keough and published in 2004, recounts experiences where institutions from different sectors find common ground in fighting poverty and improving the lives of poor communities.

Metropolitan John of Pergamon is a key figure in ecumenical dialogues between the Orthodox Church and other major Christian traditions. He is a leading theologian in the area of orthodoxy and ecology, and he has played a central role in making the Orthodox Church one of the most active religious communities in development and environmental issues. He was formerly a professor of theology at Glasgow University, Scotland, and at Kings College, London.

Archbishop Diarmuid Martin serves as Catholic Archbishop in Dublin, having been elevated to that rank in March 2001. He previously served as permanent observer of the Holy See at the UN office and specialized agencies at the World Trade Organization in Geneva. Archbishop Martin entered the service of the Holy See in 1976 in the Pontifical Council for the Family, where he was appointed undersecretary for justice and peace in 1986 and secretary in 1994. He represented the Holy See at major UN conferences on social questions and participated in activities sponsored by the World Bank and the International Monetary Fund on international debt and poverty reduction. Archbishop Martin was a member of various Vatican offices, including the Central Committee for the Great Jubilee of the Year 2000. He was also a member of the Joint Working Group for relations between the Roman Catholic Church and the World Council of Churches, and was a founding trustee of the World Faiths Development Dialogue. He led the delegations of the Holy See to the Ministerial Conference of the World Trade Organization (Doha, Qatar, 2001) and to the World Conference against Racism, Racial Discrimination, Xenophobia, and Related Intolerance (Durban, South Africa, 2001).

Marcel Massé is executive director of the World Bank for Canada, Ireland, and the Caribbean nations, a position he has held since November 2002. He was previously executive director for Canada at the Inter-American Development Bank from 1999 to 2002 and president of the Canadian International Development Agency from 1989 to 1993. Mr. Massé was also a member of the Board of Directors for Canada of the International

Monetary Fund from 1985 to 1989. He has been involved in Canadian politics since 1971, when he became economic adviser to the Privy Council office in Ottawa. From 1993 to 1999, he was a member of Parliament for Hull-Aylmer, as well as president of the Queen's Privy Council, minister of intergovernmental affairs, and minister of public service renewal. From 1996 to 1999, he was also president of the Treasury Board of Canada and minister for infrastructure. Mr. Massé worked in the World Bank's Administration and Economics Division from 1967 to 1971.

His Eminence Theodore Cardinal McCarrick was installed as Catholic Archbishop of Washington in January 2001 and was elevated to the College of Cardinals by Pope John Paul II the next month. Cardinal McCarrick is chancellor of the Catholic University of America and president of the board of trustees of the Basilica of the National Shrine of the Immaculate Conception. For the Vatican, he serves on the Pontifical Council for Justice and Peace, the Pontifical Council for the Pastoral Care of Migrants and Itinerant Peoples, and the Pontifical Commission for Latin America. He has visited many nations as a human rights advocate and to survey humanitarian needs, traveling to Sri Lanka after the tsunami in December 2004. He is an active member of the U.S. Conference of Catholic Bishops and has headed a number of its committees, including Migration (1986 and 1992), Aid to the Church in Central and Eastern Europe (1992), International Policy (1996), and Domestic Policy (2001). He was one of 15 U.S. bishops elected to the Synod for America in 1997, which examined issues of social justice in light of the new millennium. He was named a member of the U.S. Commission for International Religious Freedom in July 1999, and the president of Lebanon named him an officer of the Order of the Cedars of Lebanon in January 2000. The president of the United States presented him with the Eleanor Roosevelt Award for Human Rights later that year.

Reverend Dr. Alan McCormick is the dean of residence and Anglican chaplain at Trinity College, Dublin. He teaches theology and manages a small fund at Trinity on ecumenical affairs. He is also adviser to the Anglican Archbishop of Dublin on ecumenical affairs.

Reverend Dr. Patricia Nickson is a fellow of the School of Tropical Medicine at the University of Liverpool, United Kingdom. She has spent more than 30 years as a mission partner of the Church Mission Society, working with governments and churches in developing countries, including Afghanistan, Bangladesh, and the Democratic Republic of Congo. Following her studies, she was appointed a senior lecturer in the School of Tropical Medicine and director of the Pan-African Institute for Community Health in the Democratic Republic of Congo. Reverend Nickson uses a community-determined approach to health and development, and she has adopted this method for work on refugee and war situations in the Great Lakes area of Africa, on severe epidemics, and on health and development issues in both rural and urban areas. She was awarded the Order of the British Empire in 2005 and now spends several months a year in parish life in the Anglican Diocese of Chester.

Thoraya Obaid has been executive director of the United Nations Population Fund (UNPFA) since January 2001 and is the first Saudi national to be appointed head of a UN agency. From 1998 to 2001, she was director of the Division for Arab States and Europe at UNFPA. Preceding her work at the UNFPA, Ms. Obaid was deputy executive secretary for the Economic and Social Commission for Western Asia (ESCWA) from 1993 to 1998, chief of the Social Development and Population Division from 1992 to 1993, and senior social affairs officer from 1975 to 1992. At ESCWA, she focused on countering gender inequality as an integral part of social development programs. Helping governments establish programs to empower women has been a central focus of Ms. Obaid's work at both ESCWA and UNFPA. She is also deeply committed to the need to combat the HIV/AIDS pandemic, with particular emphasis on its implications for women and girls.

Philip O'Brien is director of the UNICEF Regional Office in Geneva. His several posts with UNICEF have included responsibility for global strategic program support to regional and country offices. He has also helped UNICEF and the World Bank collaborate on new programming. Mr. O'Brien joined UNICEF in May 1988 as chief of health and nutrition in Bangladesh. In March 1993, he was appointed UN coordinator of Southern Sector of Operation Lifeline Sudan, the support program for Southern Sudan. In June 1996, he was appointed senior program officer in UNICEF's Office of Emergency Programs, where he was responsible for providing operating and policy support to UNICEF offices working in crisis situations. Mr. O'Brien worked with Concern Worldwide, an Irish nongovernmental organization, from 1975 to 1988.

Martin Palmer is secretary general of the Alliance of Religions and Conservation (ARC). A secular body founded in 1995, ARC helps the world's major religions develop environmental programs according to their core teachings, beliefs, and practices. Mr. Palmer is a regular broadcaster on the BBC and the author of more than 30 books on world religions, ecology, development, and faith-based issues, and he is a translator of classical Daoist, Buddhist, and Christian Chinese texts. He has worked with the World Bank on a wide range of projects involving religions since 1995. Mr. Palmer is also an ambassador for the World Wildlife Fund, helping it build new partnerships to protect nature and to encourage better lifestyles worldwide.

Fr. Dominique Peccoud is special adviser on socioreligious affairs to the director-general of the International Labour Organization (ILO). He is also in charge of the relations between the ILO and civil society organizations in its External Relations and Partnerships Department. As member of both the French Academy of Agriculture and the French National Academy of Engineering, Fr. Peccoud advises the French government and nongovernmental organizations on the ethical dimensions of social and economic issues and on problems regarding the application of new technologies. Prior to joining the ILO, he was president of the Purpan Group, a graduate university for technology, civil engineering, and agriculture in Toulouse, France. He recently edited *Philosophical and Spiritual Perspectives on Decent Work*, published in 2004.

Mary Robinson is director of the Ethical Globalization Initiative, which aims to foster more equitable international trade and development, strengthen responses to HIV/AIDS in Africa, and create more humane migration policies. She is also vice president of the Club of Madrid and chairs the Council of Women World Leaders. She was UN high commissioner for human rights from 1997 to 2002, where she focused on integrating human rights concerns into all UN activities and reorienting the priorities of her office on country and regional levels. She came to the United Nations after a distinguished tenure as president of Ireland from 1990 to 1997, during which time she developed Ireland's economic, political, and cultural links with other countries and cultures, with special emphasis on the needs of developing countries. Before her presidency, Ms. Robinson served for 20 years as a senator in the Seanad Éireann, the Irish Senate. In 1969, she became the youngest Reid professor of constitutional and criminal law at Trinity College, Dublin, where she also served as lecturer in European community law. She was called to the bar in 1967, becoming a senior counsel in 1980 and a member of the English bar (middle temple) in 1973. She also served as a member of the International Commission of Jurists (1987–90) and the Advisory Commission of Inter-Rights (1984–90).

Rabbi David Rosen, former chief rabbi of Ireland, is the Jerusalem-based director of the American Jewish Committee's Department for Interreligious Affairs and of its Heilbrunn Institute for International Interreligious Understanding. He is a leading member of many international interfaith organizations, including the Council of Christians and Jews, Religions for Peace (of which he is president), and the International Advisory Committee of the Council for a Parliament of the World's Religions. Rabbi Rosen is a founder of the Inter-religious Coordinating Council in Israel, which includes some 70 organizations involved in interfaith relations. As a member of the Permanent Bilateral Commission of the State of Israel and the Holy See, he helped negotiate normalized relations between the Vatican and Israel. He serves as a member of the International Jewish Committee for Inter-religious Consultations. He is an honorary president of the International Council of Churches and Jews, the umbrella organization for more than 30 national bodies promoting Christian-Jewish relations. Rabbi Rosen was an initiator of the Alexandria Summit of leaders of the three monotheistic faiths of the Holy Land, held in Alexandria, Egypt. He is also a founding member of the World Economic Forum's

Council of 100 Leaders, which was formed to advance cooperation between the Muslim and Western worlds.

Rabbi David Saperstein directs the Religious Action Center of Reform Judaism, an organization at the center of Jewish efforts to promote social justice for more than 40 years. He represents the national Reform Jewish Movement at the U.S. Congress and has headed several national religious coalitions during his 30-year tenure as director of the center. He currently co-chairs the Coalition to Preserve Religious Liberty, which is composed of more than 60 national religious denominations and educational groups, and he serves on the boards of numerous U.S. organizations, including the National Association for the Advancement of Colored People (NAACP) and People for the American Way. In 1999, Rabbi Saperstein was elected as the first chair of the U.S. Commission on International Religious Freedom, which was created by a unanimous vote of Congress. He is an attorney and teaches at Georgetown University Law School. His articles have appeared in the *Washington Post*, the *New York Times*, and the *Harvard Law Review*.

Jean-Louis Sarbib was appointed senior vice president of the World Bank's Human Development Network in July 2003. He advises the Bank and its client countries on innovative and integrated approaches to improving health, education, and social protection, with a view to helping meet the Millennium Development Goals. Mr. Sarbib represents the Bank on a number of global initiatives, including the Global Alliance for Vaccines and Immunization, the UNAIDS Committee of Co-sponsoring Organizations, the Education for All Fast Track Initiative, and the Health Metrics Network. He also serves on several boards of international organizations involved in human development. From 2000 to 2003, Mr. Sarbib served as Bank vice president for the Middle East and North Africa Region, and from 1996 to 2000, he was the vice president for the Africa Region. After working for the French Ministry of Industry as deputy director of the Groupe de Réflexion sur les Stratégies Industrielles, he taught at the University of Pennsylvania and the University of North Carolina.

Ousmane Seck recently retired from the Islamic Development Bank (IDB) where his last position was vice president of operations; previously, he held the position of principal adviser to the president of the IDB. The IDB's purpose is to foster economic development and social progress of member countries and Muslim communities individually, as well as jointly, in accordance with the principles of Islamic law. In his role as vice president, Mr. Seck developed the Technical Cooperation Program, which is devoted to the promotion of Human Resources Development in member countries through exchange of expertise and sharing of experience. While serving as vice president of operations at the IDB, Mr. Seck was a member of the Ministerial Committee of the Intergovernmental Group of Twenty-Four on International Monetary Affairs, which is under the auspices of the International Monetary Fund.

Sahib Jathedar Manjit Singh has been a Sikh preacher for more than 26 years. He is head of the World Sikh Council in the United States, which aims to promote Sikh interests at the national and international level, and which focuses on issues of advocacy, education, and humankind. He has preached in many other countries, including Afghanistan, Canada, India, the Republic of Korea, Malaysia, Singapore, the United Kingdom, and the United States. He spends much of his time working with Sikh youth. In addition to his religious and social activities, Sahib Singh is committed to environmental preservation. He attended the Religions and Conservation Summit at Windsor Palace in 1998 and the State of the World Forum in San Francisco in September 1995, which was sponsored by the Gorbachev Foundation. He is active in several international programs geared toward achieving world peace and natural harmony. In 1993, he presided over the World Parliament of Religions in Chicago.

Rajwant Singh has been participating in Sikh community affairs since his youth and is active in issues surrounding peace, justice, and religious freedom. Mr. Singh chairs the Sikh Council on Religion and Education, which he founded in 1998. Based in Washington, D.C., the council serves as a think tank and represents Sikhs in various venues. He organized two briefings for Sikh leaders and businesspeople at the White House during the Clinton administration. From 1994 to 1996, Mr. Singh was the first Sikh president of the Interfaith Conference of Metropolitan Washington, D.C., an organization that brings together nine world religions for dialogue and joint work on critical issues. He has also served as a board member for the North American Interfaith Network since its inception. In 2000, he was a delegate to the UN Peace Summit of spiritual leaders, and he is also executive director of the Guru Gobind Singh Foundation, which conducts camps for Sikh children throughout the United States to promote Sikh culture.

Sulak Sivaraksa is a teacher, scholar, publisher, social and environmental activist, founder of many organizations, and the author of more than a hundred books and monographs in both Thai and English. In the 1960s at the age of 28, Sivaraksa founded *Sangkhomsaat Paritat* (*Social Science Review*), which quickly became a prominent intellectual publication in Thailand. During the 1970s, he became the central figure in a number of nongovernmental organizations in Thailand, where he began to develop indigenous, sustainable, and spiritual models for change. He has since expanded his work to the regional and international levels. He has co-founded the Asian Cultural Forum on Development and the International Network of Engaged Buddhists, which aims at all levels for freedom, human rights, traditional cultural integrity, social justice, and environmental protection. Sivaraksa has twice been nominated for the Nobel Peace Prize and has won the prestigious Right Livelihood Award, which honors individuals whose lives reflect high levels of personal integrity. In *Loyalty Demands Dissent*, he recounts his life as a "radical conservative"—both contemplative and activist, traditionalist and modernist, loyalist and dissident. Sivaraksa was born the year that Thailand emerged from absolute monarchy into democracy, and his life has been intimately bound up with his country's modern history. His most recent book is titled *Conflict, Culture, Change*.

Faouzi Skali is the founder and director general of the Fez Festival of World Sacred Music. He is a cultural anthropologist, ethnologist, writer, and speaker, and he has written several works on Sufism, the mystical branch of Islam. In 1994, Mr. Skali initiated the Fez Festival, an international celebration of sacred music held annually in the ancient city of Fez, Morocco, with the aim of bridging cultural divides and celebrating diversity. In 2000, Mr. Skali founded the Giving a Soul to Globalization Colloquium, the intellectual component of the festival, which examines vital global issues. The United Nations honored Mr. Skali in 2001 as one of the world's seven people who have made a major contribution to dialogue between cultures and civilizations. He was recently chosen a founding member of Comité des Sages (Group of Wise People), which advises the European Commission on education and culture. Mr. Skali is a professor at the Ecole Normale Supérieure in Fez, and his publications include *La Voie Soufi* (*The Soufi Path*), *Traces de Lumière* (*Traces of Light*), and *Le Face à Face des Coeurs: Le soufisme aujourd'hui* (*A Dialogue of Hearts: Sufism Today*).

Dame Rosemary Spencer entered the British diplomatic service in 1962. She was minister in charge of the British Embassy in Berlin from 1993 to 1996, when she helped build relations with the former East Germany and Berlin as the last British and other allied forces were leaving the city. She has also represented the United Kingdom in the European Union in Brussels, in Paris, in Lagos, in Nairobi, and several times in London. In 1996, she became British ambassador to the Netherlands and received the title dame commander of the Most Distinguished Order of St. Michael and St. George. Since retiring from the diplomatic service in 2001, she has assumed a number of functions on a voluntary basis, including serving as a trustee of the World Faiths Development Dialogue from 2002 to 2005.

Bishop Gunnar Staalsett was appointed Lutheran Bishop of Oslo, Norway, in March 1998, and since 1994, he has headed the seminary for practical theology at the University of Oslo. From 1985 to 1991 and again since 1994, Bishop Staalsett has been a member of the Nobel Peace Prize Committee. He was general secretary of the Church of Norway Council on Ecumenical and International Relations from 1970 to 1977, general secretary of the Norwegian Bible Society from 1982 to 1985, and general secretary of the Lutheran World Federation from 1985 to 1994. He chairs Norwegian Church Aid, an independent, ecumenical development aid organization. Bishop Staalsett has been involved in politics since 1992, serving as chair of the Norwegian Center Party (Senterpartiet) from 1977 to 1979 and then as deputy member of Parliament from 1979 to 1982. He has been a member of the executive committees of the World Council of Churches and the Norwegian UNESCO Committee and served on the Advisory Board on Development and HIV/AIDS of the Norwegian government. He has received many awards and published widely.

Reverend William Vendley has served since 1994 as secretary general of Religions for Peace, the world's largest organization dedicated solely to promoting collaboration among religious communities. Reverend Vendley is a member of the Governing Board of Religions for Peace, and he also serves as the organization's chief executive officer, overseeing the international secretariat in North America, Europe, the Balkans, West and East Africa, and Asia. He coordinates the international projects of Religions for Peace's Inter-religious Councils in 50 countries. Under Reverend Vendley's leadership, Religions for Peace and its local affiliates have helped mediate conflicts in the Balkans, West Africa, and the Horn of Africa, and have supported the work of religious communities relating to AIDS orphans in Africa. Under his leadership, Religions for Peace also established the Global Network of Religious Women's Organizations, which facilitates collaboration among these groups and mainstreams them into Religions for Peace's action programs. Reverend Vendley is a theologian and has served as a professor and dean at graduate schools of theology. He lectures frequently in academic, UN, and NGO forums. He has received several prizes related to religion and human rights, and he serves on the boards of organizations concerned with topics from fine arts to peace building.

Matthew Weinberg was formerly executive director of the Institute for Studies in Global Prosperity, a research agency of the Bahá'í International Community. He was previously a senior analyst with the U.S. Congressional Office of Technology Assessment in Washington, D.C., where he directed studies in environmental, energy, and technology policy. He is the author of publications on public policy, social and economic development, science and ethics, human rights, and religious tolerance.

James D. Wolfensohn, ninth president of the World Bank Group, established his career as an international investment banker with a parallel involvement in development issues and the global environment. In September 1999, Mr. Wolfensohn was reappointed to a second five-year team as Bank president, beginning in June 2000. He is the third president in the Bank's history to have served a second term and is retiring in May 2005. Since becoming president in June 1995, Mr. Wolfensohn has traveled to more than 100 countries to gain firsthand experience with the challenges facing the World Bank. He has visited Bank-supported development projects and met with client governments and representatives from business, labor, media, and nongovernmental organizations; religious and women's groups; students; and teachers. He has formed new strategic partnerships between the Bank and the governments it serves, the private sector, civil society organizations, regional development banks, and the United Nations. Mr. Wolfensohn has placed sustainable poverty reduction at the center of the Bank's mission and has focused on supporting the international effort to reach the Millennium Development Goals. He has called on rich donor nations to increase foreign development assistance, harmonize aid processes, and lower trade barriers to fulfill those goals. He has also urged developing countries to implement key policy reforms to promote growth, reduce poverty, and deliver quality health care and schooling to all citizens. Before joining the Bank, Mr. Wolfensohn was president and chief executive officer of James D. Wolfensohn Inc., the investment firm he founded in 1981. He was born in Australia and is a naturalized U.S. citizen. In May 1995, Queen Elizabeth II bestowed on him an honorary knighthood for his contributions to the arts.

The Most Venerable Master Sheng Yen is credited with sparking a revival of Chinese Buddhism. He has taught throughout Asia, Europe, North America, and Eastern Europe. Master Sheng Yen not only is an internationally renowned Chan master but also has a strong background in scholarship. He seeks to demonstrate that Chan practice can benefit society through its diverse service and community-orientated activities. Through intensive meditation, dharma talks, and work, practitioners from around the world engage their minds and hearts to develop inner stillness, concentration, and a deeper understanding of themselves, others, and the world. Grounded in this wisdom, they engage the world with great concern, compassion, and kindness. Owing to Master Sheng Yen's involvement with promoting peace and his bearing and tolerance as a religious leader, he has been invited to numerous international conferences and meetings. In 1998, he engaged in a three-day dialogue with his Holiness the Dalai Lama in New York. In August 2000, he attended the UN Millennium World Peace Summit of Religious and Spiritual Leaders, where he delivered a keynote speech. He also attended the 2002 World Economic Forum in New York.

(*l to r*) Canon Richard Marsh, Sulak Sivaraksa, Lord George Carey

Acknowledgments

F inding Global Balance is the third book resulting from the work of the Development Dialogue on Values and Ethics Unit in the World Bank, following *Millennium Challenges for Development and Faith Institutions* and *Mind, Heart, and Soul in the Fight Against Poverty.* All three pay tribute to the contributions of faith leaders and organizations that are fighting poverty and improving the lives of the world's poor and marginalized people, and all three highlight the scope for enhanced partnerships between the worlds of faith and development. This book comes out of the fourth meeting of faith and development leaders, held January 31 and February 1, 2005, in Dublin, Ireland, a remarkable gathering of leaders who deliberated openly, honestly, and thoughtfully about the critical issues facing our world, and about the prospects for greater collaboration between the faith and development leaders and organizations in eradicating poverty, improving access to social services, and promoting greater global equity and social justice.

The Dublin meeting and this publication reflect shared efforts from within the Bank and outside. Prior to the meeting, Katherine Marshall and Lucy Keough led a team within the Bank, including Olivia Donnelly, Jan-Marie Hopkins, Rebecca Ling, Desmond McCarthy, Lilia Tolentino, and Marisa Van Saanen, who contributed to the preparation and coordination of background papers for the Dublin meeting. Jodi Lehner provided invaluable overall logistical management. Following the conclusion of the Dublin meeting, Marisa Van Saanen has contributed significantly to the preparation of this book. In addition, Sandra Hackman and Olivia Donnelly have provided critical editorial support and other contributions. Mark Ingebretsen guided the book through the production process with care and aplomb.

This book would not have been possible without the help of many outside of the Bank, including, critically, the cochairs of the Dublin meeting, Lord George Carey and Archbishop Diarmuid Martin. Both of them contributed their time and their teams to make possible the meeting in Dublin and this subsequent publication. Special thanks must go to Father Paul Tighe, Annette O'Donnell, Ersilia Davidson, and Christine West in Archbishop Martin's office.

We would also like to thank each and every participant in the Dublin meeting, each of whom demonstrated remarkable levels of insight, commitment, and passion throughout all their deliberations. This book reflects progress in bridging gaps between the worlds of faith and development, but much work is ahead. This book is dedicated to bringing together religious and development leaders to *find global balance in a world characterized by equity and social justice.* The task is a daunting one—the challenge of our generation—and we contend it is much better when approached in partnership.

Abbreviations
and Acronyms

ABC model	Abstinence, Being faithful, and responsible use of Condoms
AIDS	Acquired Immunodeficiency Syndrome
ARC	Alliance of Religions and Conservation
ARVs	Antiretrovirals
CBO	Community-based Organization
ESCWA	Economic and Social Commission for Western Asia
HIV	Human Immunodeficiency Virus
ICCJ	International Council of Churches and Jews
ILO	International Labour Organization
IMF	International Monetary Fund
MDGs	Millennium Development Goals
NGO	Nongovernmental organization
OECD	Organisation for Economic Co-operation and Development
UN	United Nations
UNAIDS	Joint United Nations Programs on HIV/AIDS
UNDP	United Nations Development Program
UNESCO	United Nations Educational, Scientific, and Cultural Organization
UNICEF	The United Nations Children's Fund
WCC	World Council of Churches
WCRP	World Conference of Religions for Peace (known today as "Religions for Peace")
WDR	World Development Report
WEF	World Economic Forum
WFDD	World Faiths Development Dialogue
WFP	World Food Programme
WHO	World Health Organization

Selected Bibliography

Belshaw, Deryke, Robert Calderisi, and Christopher Sugden, eds. *Faith in Development: Partnership Between the World Bank and the Churches of Africa*. London: Regnum Press, 2001.

Byamugisha, Gideon, Lucy Y. Steinitz, Glen Williams, and Phumzile Zondi. *Journeys of Faith: Church-based Responses to HIV and AIDS in Three Southern African Countries*. St. Albans, U.K.: Teaching-aids At Low Cost (TALC), 2002.

Catholic Medical Mission Board and Global Health Council. "Faith in Action: Examining the Role of Faith Based Organizations in Addressing HIV/AIDS." Washington, DC: Catholic Medical Mission Board and Global Health Council, 2005. http://www.globalhealth.org/images/pdf/faith_in_action/faith_in_action_final.pdf.

Collier, Paul, V. L. Elliot, Havard Hegre, Anke Hoeffler, Marta Reynal-Querol, and Nicholas Sambanis. *Breaking the Conflict Trap: Civil War and Development Policy*. Policy Research Report. New York: Oxford University Press, 2003.

Keough, Lucy. "Conquering 'Slim': Uganda's War on HIV/AIDS." Global Learning Process on Scaling Up Poverty Reduction, Shanghai Conference, May 25–27, 2004.

Kung, Hans. *World Religions, Universal Peace, Global Ethic*. Tübingen, Germany: Institute for Global Ethics, 2002.

Marshall, Katherine. "Development and Religion: A Different Lens on Development Debates." *Peabody Journal of Education* 76 (3 & 4): 339–75.

Marshall, Katherine, and Lucy Keough, eds. *Mind, Heart, and Soul in the Fight Against Poverty*. Washington, DC: World Bank, 2004.

Marshall, Katherine, and Richard Marsh, eds. *Millennium Challenges for Faith and Development Institutions*. Washington, DC: World Bank, 2003.

Mshana, Rogate, ed. "In Search of Just Economy: Common Goals, Separate Journeys, The Second Encounter of the World Council of Churches, World Bank, and International Monetary Fund, Washington, DC, 28–29 October 2003." Geneva: WCC Publications, 2004.

Narayan, Deepa, Raj Patel, Kai Schafft, Anne Rademacher, and Sarah Kock-Schulte. *Voices of the Poor: Can Anyone Hear Us?* New York: Oxford University Press, 2000.

Palmer, Martin, with Victoria Finlay. *Faith in Conservation: New Approaches to Religions and the Environment.* Washington, DC: World Bank, 2003.

Sen, Amartya. *Development as Freedom.* New York: Anchor Books, 1999.

Sivaraksa, Sulak. *Conflict, Culture, Change: Engaged Buddhism in a Globalizing World.* Somerville, MA: Wisdom Publications, 2005.

UN General Assembly, Fifth-ninth Session. *In Larger Freedom: Towards Development, Security, and Human Rights for All.* Report of the Secretary General, A/59/2005, 21 March 2005. Available at http://www.un.org/largerfreedom/report-largerfreedom.pdf.

UN Millennium Project (Jeffrey Sachs, dir.). "Investing in Development: A Practical Plan to Achieve the Millennium Development Goals." New York: Earthscan, 2005. http://www.unmillenniumproject.org/reports/index.htm.

UNAIDS (Joint United Nations Programme on AIDS). *AIDS Epidemic Update December 2004.* Geneva: UNAIDS, 2004.

World Bank. *Post-Conflict Reconstruction: The Role of the World Bank.* Washington, DC: World Bank, 1998.

_____. *World Development Report 2000/2001: Attacking Poverty.* New York: Oxford University Press, 2000.

_____. *Global Monitoring Report 2005: Millennium Development Goals: From Consensus to Momentum.* Washington, DC: World Bank, 2005. Available at http://siteresources.worldbank.org/GLOBALMONITORINGEXT/Resources/complete.pdf.

World Bank Development Dialogue on Values and Ethics Website. http://www.worldbank.org/developmentdialogue.

World Faiths Development Dialogue. *Cultures, Spirituality and Development.* Oxford, U.K.: World Faiths Development Dialogue, 2001.

_____. *Poverty and Development: An Interfaith Perspective.* Oxford, U.K.: World Faiths Development Dialogue, 1999.

World Faiths Development Dialogue Website. http://www.wfdd.org.U.K./.

Dinner reception, Haruhisa Handa

ECO-AUDIT
ENVIRONMENTAL BENEFITS STATEMENT

The World Bank is committed to preserving endangered forests and natural resources. We have chosen to print *Finding Global Balance: Common Ground between the Worlds of Development and Faith*, 10% post-consumer recycled fiber paper, processed chlorine free. The World Bank has formally agreed to follow the recommended standards for paper usage set by the Green Press Initiative, a nonprofit program supporting publishers in using fiber that is not sourced from endangered forests. For more information, visit www.greenpressinitiative.org.

The printing of these books on recycled paper saved the following:

3.6	trees*
170	pounds of solid waste
1,539	gallons of water
333	pounds of net greenhouse gases
619	kilowatt hours of electricity

*40' in height. 6–8 inches in diameter.